# Internet Legal Forms For Business

J. Dianne Brinson and

Mark F. Radcliffe

Ladera Press

Credits:
The Roberts Group, editing, book design, and production
Katherine C. Spelman and Jason D. Firth, Form 12

Copyright 1997 by J. Dianne Brinson and Mark F. Radcliffe.
All rights reserved.

Some of the material in this book was previously published in the book *Multimedia Law and Business Handbook* by the same authors (Ladera Press 1996).

No part of this book may be reproduced, stored in a retrieval system, or transmitted in any form or by any means—electronic, mechanical, photocopying, recording, or otherwise—except as stated in the *Introduction* without the prior written permission of the copyright owners. Requests for permission or further information should be sent to Publisher, Ladera Press, 3130 Alpine Road, Suite 200-9002, Menlo Park, Ca. 94025.

This publication is designed to provide accurate and authoritative information in regard to the subject matter covered. It is sold with the understanding that the publisher is not engaged in rendering legal, accounting, or other professional service. If legal advice or other expert assistance is required, the services of a competent professional person should be sought.

All products or services mentioned are trademarks or service marks of their respective owners.

Printed in the U.S.A.

Publisher's Cataloging in Publication
*(provided by Quality Books Inc.)*

Brinson, J. Dianne.
    Internet legal forms for business / J. Dianne Brinson, Mark F. Radcliffe. -- 1st ed.
    p. cm.
    Preassigned LCCN: 97-71372
    ISBN: 0-9639173-4-X

    1. Commercial law--United States--Forms. 2. Forms (Law)--United States--Computer network resources. 3. Internet (Computer network) I. Radcliffe, Mark F. II. Title

KF886.B75 1997        025.06'346
                            QBI97-40910

# Contents

**Introduction** v

**Overview** 1
- *Copyright Law* 2
- *Copyright Ownership* 8
- *Copyright Licenses* 10
- *Other Intellectual Property Laws* 13
- *Privacy And Defamation Law* 16
- *Contracts Law* 19
- *Sales Law* 20

**1 Development and Transfer Agreement** 27
- *Checklist of Issues* 28
- *Negotiating Tips: Client* 29
- *Negotiating Tips: Contractor* 30
- COPYRIGHT DEVELOPMENT AND TRANSFER AGREEMENT 32

**2 Content License** 37
- *Checklist Of Issues* 38
- *Negotiating Tips: Licensee* 39
- *Negotiating Tips: Licensor* 40
- TEXT LICENSE AGREEMENT 43

**3 Content License** 47
- *Checklist Of Issues* 48
- *Negotiating Tips: Licensee* 50
- *Negotiating Tips: Licensor* 51
- PHOTO AND VIDEO FOOTAGE LICENSE AGREEMENT 53

**4 Web Site Terms and Conditions of Use** 57
- *Checklist Of Issues* 58
- WEB SITE TERMS AND CONDITIONS OF USE 61

**5 Privacy Release** 65
- *Checklist Of Issues* 66
- *Negotiating Tips: Grantee* 66
- *Negotiating Tips: Grantor* 67
- PRIVACY RELEASE 68

## 6 Web Site Development Agreement   69
*Checklist Of Issues   70*
*Negotiating Tips: Client   72*
*Negotiating Tips: Developer   74*
WEB SITE DEVELOPMENT AND MAINTENANCE AGREEMENT   76

## 7 Internet Advertising Contract   89
*Checklist Of Issues   90*
*Negotiating Tips: Host Provider   92*
*Negotiating Tips: Customer   92*
INTERNET ADVERTISING CONTRACT   94

## 8 Chat Room Agreement   99
CHAT ROOM AGREEMENT   101

## 9 Internet Use Policy   103
INTERNET USE POLICY   105

## 10 Clickwrap Agreement   107
*Checklist Of Issues For Seller/Licensor   108*
CLICKWRAP AGREEMENT   110

## 11 Linking Agreements   113
*Form 11A Permission To Link   115*
*Checklist Of Issues   115*
PERMISSION TO LINK   117
*Form 11B Linking Agreement (Revenue-sharing)   118*
*Checklist Of Issues   118*
*Negotiating Tips: Licensor   119*
*Negotiating Tips: Licensee   120*
LINKING AGREEMENT   122

## 12 Domain Name Assignment Agreement   131
*Geographic Domain Names   133*
*Global Domain Names   133*
*Possible Changes   134*
*Domain Name Disputes   134*
*Network Solutions Dispute Resolution Policy   134*
*Establishing Strong Domain Name Rights   135*
*Domain Name Transfers   137*
DOMAIN NAME ASSIGNMENT AGREEMENT   139

# Introduction

Legal issues are critical to success when doing business on the Internet. Legal mistakes can cost you thousands of dollars in damages and attorneys' fees.

This book provides form contracts for setting up and running a business online. It includes a Web site development contract, content licenses, an advertising agreement, Web site terms and conditions of use, a clickwrap license, and other necessary contracts for doing business on the Internet. With each contract, we've included information on why the contract is needed, an issues checklist, and negotiating tips. We've also included an Overview of Internet Legal Issues to help you understand why the contracts are necessary.

You may photocopy or scan these contracts for your personal use in your business or law practice or use by your company. A diskette version of the forms is available for $12 (order information is at the end of the book). The forms may not be reproduced or modified for use by third parties without the permission of the authors.

We would like to thank Katherine C. Spelman and Jason D. Firth of Steinhart & Falconer, San Francisco, for providing Form 12. Thanks also to Gray Cary Ware & Freidenrich and to Margo Komenar, of Komenar Production & Marketing Group, Tiburon, California.

This book includes our opinions. They should not be interpreted as those of Gray Cary Ware & Freidenrich or its clients. We have done our best to accurately reflect the practices in this rapidly evolving industry, but any errors are solely our responsibility.

The contracts in this book should be considered samples rather than "model" agreements that will fit all your needs. You should review them and the accompanying material carefully to understand the issues that you need to address.

These contracts may not fit your needs in a particular transaction. Consult with an experienced attorney prior to using any of these contracts.

# Overview

# Internet Legal Issues

THERE REALLY IS NO SUCH THING AS "INTERNET LAW." Instead, there are a number of laws that apply to things that are done on the Internet. In this brief Overview, we'll discuss several laws that are important for doing business on the Internet. Here are the laws we'll cover:

- Copyright
- Copyright Ownership
- Copyright Licenses
- Other Intellectual Property Laws
- Privacy and Defamation
- Contracts
- Sales

Our coverage of each law is brief and limited to United States law. For fuller coverage of U.S. law on these topics, consult our book *Multimedia Law and Business Handbook* (see the order form at the end of this book).

There are many laws in addition to the ones discussed here that apply to activities on the Internet—for example, criminal laws, obscenity laws, consumer protection laws, laws regulating advertising, and export control laws. For information on laws not covered in this book and on other countries' laws, please consult other publications or your attorney.

## Copyright Law

Contrary to what some people think, copyright law applies to the Internet. If you copy copyrighted graphics, text, photos, or music and use that material in your Web site without permission, you are opening yourself up to a lawsuit for copyright infringement.

### Copyright Basics

Found some great content for your Web site? Chances are that it's protected by copyright. Here's why:

- Copyright protection is available for text, art, graphics, photos, and music (both compositions and recordings) and is easy to obtain.
- Copyright protection lasts a long time. The copyright term for a work created by an individual after January 1, 1978 is the life of the author plus 50 years. For a work created by an employee within the scope of the employment after January 1, 1978—"work made for hire"—the term is 75 years from the date of first "publication" (distribution of copies to the general public) or 100 years from the date of creation, whichever expires first.

You may be familiar with copyright registration and copyright notice. Under current U.S. law, registration and notice are optional. Copyright protection arises automatically when an "original" work of authorship is "fixed" in a tangible medium of expression.

A work is "original" as long as it owes its origin to the author (as opposed to being copied from some preexisting work). A work can be original without being novel, unique, creative, or valuable. A work is "fixed" when it is made "sufficiently permanent or stable to permit it to be perceived, reproduced, or communicated for a period of more than transitory duration." Forms of "fixation" include writing, typing, dictating into a tape recorder, entering into a computer, and videotaping.

### The Copyright Owner's Rights

Before you use copyrighted material owned by a third party on your Web site, you should determine whether it is necessary to obtain permission from the owner. For most uses, permission should be obtained.

You need permission if your use of the material without permission would violate one of the copyright owner's five exclusive rights in the copyrighted work. Those rights are as follows:

- ***Reproduction Right.*** The reproduction right is the right to copy, duplicate, transcribe, or imitate the work in fixed form. Scanning is one way of exercising the reproduction right.

- ***Modification Right.*** The modification right (also known as the derivative works right) is the right to modify the work to create a new work. A new work that is based on a preexisting work is known as a "derivative work." Altering a photograph is an exercise of the modification right, as is creating an interactive version of a novel.

- ***Distribution Right.*** The distribution right is the right to distribute copies of the work to the public by sale, rental, lease, or lending.

- ***Public Performance Right.*** The public performance right is the right to recite, play, dance, act, or show the work at a public place or to transmit it to the public. In the case of a motion picture or other audiovisual work, showing the work's images in sequence is considered "performance." Sound recordings—recorded versions of music or other sounds—do not have a public performance right except for a special "digital performance right," a license to which would be required to use a sound recording on the Internet.

- ***Public Display Right.*** The public display right is the right to show a copy of the work directly or by means of a film, slide, or television image at a public place or to transmit it to the public. In the case of a motion picture or other audiovisual work, showing the work's images out of sequence is considered "display." Making material available for Internet users to look at on your Web site is considered public display.

Anyone who violates any of the exclusive rights of a copyright owner is an infringer.

> **Example:** *John scanned Photographer's copyrighted photograph, altered the image by using digital editing software, and included the altered version of the photograph in John's Web site. If John used Photographer's photograph without permission, John infringed Photographer's copyright by violating the reproduction right (scanning the photograph), the modification right (altering the photograph), and the public display right.*

A copyright owner can recover actual, or in some cases, statutory damages from an infringer. Those who use infringing material provided by others can also be liable for infringement.

**Example:** *Suppose John (in the example above) was a Web site developer who used Photographer's photo in a Web site which John created for Client. Client's use of the photo in Client's Web site makes Client an infringer, too (even if Client had no intent to infringe and didn't know that John used Photographer's photo without permission).*

In Forms 1, 2, 3, and 6, we remind you that you can be liable for copyright infringement for using material prepared for you by others, and we recommend things you can do to protect yourself.

Employers are liable for infringement done by their employees within the scope of the employment. Whether a system operator, Internet service provider, bulletin board provider, Web site provider, or Chat Room provider is liable when someone using the operator's or provider's facilities commits copyright infringement through those facilities is currently being debated.

Forms 4, 8, and 9 include provisions to help protect employers, Chat Room providers, and Web site providers from liability for infringement by employees and users.

## Avoiding Infringement

How can you use copyrighted material without running the risk of being sued for infringement? Get permission—known as a "license"—from the copyright owner. Licenses are discussed in a later section of this Overview.

There are a number of myths concerning the necessity of getting a license. Here are five. Don't make the mistake of believing them:

■ *Myth #1: "The work I want to use doesn't have a copyright notice on it, so it's not copyrighted. I'm free to use it."*

Most published works contain a copyright notice. However, for works published on or after March 1, 1989, the use of copyright notice is optional. The fact that a work doesn't have a copyright notice doesn't mean that the work is not protected by copyright. This statement is true for material you find on the Internet, too. While you are free to copy and use public domain material (discussed later in this section of the Overview) that you find on the Net, much of the material on the Net is protected by copyright—whether or not it has a copyright notice on it.

And Web sites themselves are protected by copyright as "compilations" of preexisting material.

■ *Myth #2: "I don't need a license because I'm using only a small amount of the copyrighted work."*

It is true that *de minimis* copying (copying a small amount) is not copyright infringement. Unfortunately, it is rarely possible to tell where *de minimis* copying ends and copyright infringement begins. There are no "bright line" rules.

Copying a small amount of a copyrighted work is infringement if what is copied is a qualitatively substantial portion of the copied work. In one case, a magazine article that used 300 words from a 200,000-word autobiography written by President Gerald Ford was found to infringe the copyright on the autobiography. Even though the copied material was only a small part of the autobiography, the copied portions were among the most powerful passages in the autobiography. Copying any part of a copyrighted work is risky. If what you copy is truly a tiny and nonmemorable part of the work, you may get away with it (the work's owner may not be able to tell that your work incorporates an excerpt from the owner's work). However, you run the risk of having to defend your use in expensive litigation. If you are copying, it is better to get a permission or a license (unless fair use applies). You cannot escape liability for infringement by showing how much of the protected work you did not take.

■ *Myth #3: "Since I'm planning to give credit to all authors whose works I copy, I don't need to get licenses."*

If you give credit to a work's author, you are not a plagiarist (you are not pretending that you authored the copied work). However, attribution is not a defense to copyright infringement.

■ *Myth #4: "My Web site will be a wonderful showcase for the copyright owner's work, so I'm sure the owner will not object to my use of the work."*

Don't assume that a copyright owner will be happy to have you use his or her work. Even if the owner is willing to let you use the work, the owner may want to charge you a license fee. Content owners view the Internet as a new market for licensing their material.

■ *Myth #5: "I don't need a license because I'm going to alter the work I copy."*

Generally, you cannot escape liability for copyright infringement by altering or modifying the work you copy. If you copy and modify protected elements of a copyrighted work, you will be infringing the copyright owner's modification right as well as the reproduction right.

## When You Don't Need a License

You don't need a license to use a copyrighted work in two circumstances: (1) if your use is fair use; (2) if the material you use is factual or an idea. And you don't need a license to use works that are in the public domain.

## Fair Use

You don't need permission to use a copyrighted work if your use is "fair use." The "fair use" of a copyrighted work is not an infringement of copyright. Copyright owners are, by law, deemed to consent to the fair use of their works by others. Examples of fair use are quoting passages from a book in a book review; summarizing an article, with brief quotations, for a news report; and copying a small part of a work to give to students to illustrate a lesson.

Unfortunately, it is difficult to tell whether a particular use of a work is fair or unfair. Determinations are made on a case-by-case basis by considering four factors:

- *Factor #1: Purpose and character of use.* The courts are most likely to find fair use where the use is for noncommercial purposes, such as a book review.

- *Factor #2: Nature of the copyrighted work.* The courts are most likely to find fair use where the copied work is a factual work rather than a creative one.

- *Factor #3: Amount and substantiality of the portion used.* The courts are most likely to find fair use where what is used is a tiny amount of the protected work. If what is used is small in amount but substantial in terms of importance, a finding of fair use is unlikely.

- *Factor #4: Effect on the potential market for or value of the protected work.* The courts are most likely to find fair use where the new work is not a substitute for the copyrighted work.

There's been some confusion about how fair use applies to the Internet. Some people think that using someone else's copyrighted material on the Internet is fair use, because the "culture" of the Internet is that it's okay to do this ("everyone does it"). And some think that copying and using material that you find on the Internet is also fair use. However, under current law, there is no absolute fair use right to post someone else's copyrighted material on the Internet or to use material you find on the Internet. If copyrighted material is used on the Internet or copied from the Internet without the owner's permission, whether the use is fair use will be decided by considering the four factors discussed above.

Because getting a license to use copyrighted material can be complicated and costly, you may be tempted to skip the licensing process and just rely on fair use. Before you yield to that temptation, please consider these guidelines:

- If you are creating a Web site for purely noncommercial purposes—for a nonprofit organization to use in providing information, for example—it is possible that you can justify copying small amounts of material as fair use.
- If you use copyrighted content on a Web site for a for-profit company—even an "information only" Web site—or on a Web site that serves any commercial use, it will be hard to succeed on a fair use defense. It's better to get permission.
- If your Web site serves traditional "fair use" purposes—criticism, comment, news reporting, teaching, scholarship, and research—you have a better chance of falling within the bounds of fair use than you do if your Web site's purpose is entertainment or business.

## Ideas or Facts

You don't need a license to copy facts from a protected work or to copy ideas from a protected work. The copyright on a work does not extend to the work's facts. This is because copyright protection is limited to original works of authorship, and no one can claim originality or authorship for facts. You are free to copy facts from a copyrighted work.

## Public Domain

You don't need a license to use a public domain work. Public domain works—works not protected by copyright—an be used by anyone. Because these works are not protected by copyright, no one can claim the exclusive rights of copyright for such works. For example, the plays of Shakespeare are in the public domain.

Works enter the public domain in several ways: because the term of the copyright expired, because the copyright owner failed to "renew" his copyright under the old Copyright Act of 1909, or because the copyright owner failed to properly use copyright notice (of importance only for works created before March 1, 1989, at which time copyright notice became optional). The rules regarding what works are in the public domain are too complex for this Overview, and they vary from country to country. Material that is in the public domain in this country may be protected by copyright in other countries.

The only easy-to-apply rule for determining when works are in the public domain is that a copyright that was in existence before January 1, 1978 and was renewed has a term of 75 years (and terms always run to the end of the calendar year). Consequently, in 1997, all works first "published" before January 1, 1922 are in the public domain in the United States.

Works created by federal government officers and employees as part of their official duties are not protected by copyright. This rule does not apply to works created by state government officers and employees.

## Copyright Ownership

Are you planning to hire a freelancer to create content for your Web site? Or are you planning to hire a Web site developer to create a Web site for you? Or perhaps you have employees who will be creating a Web site or Web site content for you? Or do you create material for others to use on their Web sites?

If your answer to any of these questions is "yes," you need to understand copyright law's ownership rules. The Copyright Act has "default rules" on ownership which apply if the parties to a transaction do not reach their own agreement on ownership. We'll discuss these rules here. They can always be varied by agreement of the parties.

The basic rule is that ownership of copyright initially belongs to the author or authors of the work.

> **Example:** *Sarah, a photographer, took a photograph of the Lincoln Memorial. Sarah is the author of the photograph and the initial owner of the copyright in the photograph.*

The "author" is generally the individual who created the work. However, when an employee creates work within the scope of the employment, the employer is considered the "author." Unless the parties have agreed otherwise in a signed written document, the employer owns the copyright of a work made for hire.

> **Example:** *As part of his job, John, an employee of Big Company's marketing department, created a Web site for Big Company. Even though John created the Web site, Big Company is the author for copyright purposes. Big Company owns the copyright in the Web site (unless John and Big Company have agreed in a signed contract that John owns the copyright).*

A different rule applies, however, when an independent contractor (freelancer) creates material for a client. When a hiring party and an independent contractor fail to address the issue of ownership of copyrights in works created by the independent contractor, the copyrights are owned by the independent contractor.

> **Example:** *•Client hired Freelance Graphic Designer on a project basis to create graphics for Client's Web site. If Client and Designer did not address the issue of copyright ownership, Designer owns the copyright in the graphics—even though Client paid Designer to create them.*

There are two ways for a party who hires an independent contractor to obtain ownership of the material created by the contractor:

(1) A written, signed assignment, which is a transfer of copyright ownership.

(2) A written, signed work for hire agreement, which can only be used for works commissioned for use as:

- A contribution to a collective work.
- Part of a motion picture or other audiovisual work.
- A translation.
- A supplementary work.
- A compilation.
- An instructional text.
- A test or answer material for a test.
- An atlas.

Because a work for hire agreement can only be used for contributions to these types of works—and because these agreements have other limitations—we recommend that you get an assignment if you want to get copyright ownership of material created for you by a freelancer. Form 1 and Form 6 both include assignment provisions.

Many people think that a hiring party who commissions and pays for material automatically owns the copyright in the material created by a freelancer. That's wrong.

## Assignments

When a copyright is assigned, the assignee (individual or company to whom it is assigned) becomes the owner of the exclusive rights of copyright in the protected work.

> **Example:** *Tom, an individual working on his own, created search engine software and then assigned the copyright in the software to Software Company. After the assignment, Software Company has the exclusive right to reproduce and distribute the software. If Tom starts selling the software, he will be infringing Software Company's rights as copyright owner.*

The ownership of copyright may be transferred in whole or in part. Examples of partial transfers are an assignment of the copyright for a term of 10 years (time limitation) and an assignment limited to California (geographic limitation). In addition, the individual exclusive rights (reproduction, modification, and so forth) can be transferred. Assignments are common in many industries—for example, music composers often assign copyrights in their compositions to music publishers.

An assignment is not valid unless it is in writing and is signed by the owner of the rights conveyed or the owner's authorized agent. An assignment can be recorded in the Copyright Office to give others "constructive notice" of the assignment. Constructive notice is a legal term that means you are presumed to know a fact (because it is a matter of public record) even if you have no actual knowledge of the fact.

### Owning a Copy

Copyright law distinguishes the ownership of a copy of a protected work (a print of a photograph, a compact disc, a book, a diskette) from ownership of the intangible copyright rights. The transfer of a copy of a work does not transfer any rights in the copyright. Thus, purchasing a book (a copy of a literary work, in copyright terminology) does not give you permission to make copies of the book or to post parts of the book on your Web site. You *do* have a right to resell (distribute) that copy. This exception to the copyright owner's rights is known as the "first sale doctrine."

## Copyright Licenses

A license is a copyright owner's grant of permission to use a copyrighted work in a way that would otherwise be copyright infringement. A copyright owner who grants a license is known as a licensor. A party receiving a license is known as a licensee.

A copyright license can be exclusive or nonexclusive. An exclusive license is a license that does not overlap another grant of rights.

> **Example:** *Author granted Publisher the exclusive right to sell Author's novel in the United States. She granted Movie Developer the exclusive right to create and distribute a movie version of the novel. Both Publisher and Developer have exclusive licenses. There is no overlap between the two licenses.*

Under copyright law, an exclusive license is considered a transfer of copyright ownership. An exclusive license, like an assignment, is not valid unless it is in writing and signed by the owner of the rights conveyed. A nonexclusive license is valid even if it is not in writing (but you should always get a license in writing so you'll have proof of the license and its terms).

The content licenses in this book are nonexclusive.

### Getting a License

You'll find two content license agreement forms in this book, Form 2, for licensing text, and Form 3, for licensing photos and video footage. However, before you start filling out forms, you need to determine who owns the copyright in the material you want to use and determine what rights you need.

## Finding the Owner

If the work you want to use contains a copyright notice (many works do, although use of copyright notice is now optional), the name on the notice is your starting point for locating the copyright owner. The name in the notice is the name of the copyright owner at the time the copy of the work containing that notice was published—but not necessarily the work's creator or the current copyright owner.

The copyright owner named in the notice may have assigned the copyright to someone else after your copy was published. You need to get permission from the current owner.

If the copyright in the work has been registered with the U.S. Copyright Office, one way to find the current owner is to request an "assignment search" from the Copyright Office. Such a search costs $20 per hour. For more information, contact the Copyright Office at (202) 707-3000 or visit the Copyright Office's Web site at http://lcweb.loc.gov/copyright. Information also is available by fax-on-demand at (202) 707-2600.

Getting permission to use material you find on the Internet can be particularly tricky. If you want to use material posted by someone other than the copyright owner, but with the owner's permission, you need permission from the owner, not from the poster.

> **Example:** *Online Service Provider got Author's permission to post a chapter from Author's new book on OSP's commercial online service. If Big Company wants to use part of the chapter on its Web site, Big Company needs permission from Author (not from OSP).*

Getting permission to use material you find on the Net is complicated by the fact that some people post copyrighted material they do not own, without getting permission from the copyright owner. If someone has posted copyrighted material in violation of the copyright owner's exclusive rights, getting the poster's permission to use the copyrighted material will do you no good. The poster has no right to authorize you to use the material. You need the owner's permission.

> **Example:** *John, a fan of the cartoon strip "Peanuts," used an image of Snoopy on his Web site without getting permission from the copyright owner. Sue saw Snoopy on John's Web site and wants to use the image on her Web site. Getting permission to copy Snoopy from John is worthless, since John does not own the copyright (and is himself probably an infringer of the owner's exclusive rights).*

Do not assume that the person who posted a document on the Internet is the owner. Ask questions: Who created the document? What is its origin? If there's any doubt about whether the person who put the document up is the owner, don't use the document.

If the work you want to use incorporates several different copyrightable works, you may need more than one license.

> **Example:** *Web Publisher wants to use text and an illustration from Bookco's book in an online magazine. Bookco does not own the copyright on the illustration, the freelance artist who created the illustration does (Bookco just has the artist's permission to use the illustration). To use the text and the illustration, Web needs permission from Bookco and the artist.*

If you want to use a photograph or video footage that prominently features a copyrighted work—particularly a work of fine art such as a sculpture or painting—you may need to obtain a license from the featured work's copyright owner. Because ownership of the copyright in a work is distinct from ownership of a copy, the owner of the copy of the work is probably not the copyright owner for the work.

> **Example:** *Mr. Rich gave Web site Developer permission to photograph several copyrighted paintings from Mr. Rich's private art collection and use the photographs in Developer's Web site design projects. Unless Mr. Rich owns the copyrights in the paintings, Developer should get permission to use the images of the paintings from the copyright owners (the artists, most likely).*

## Determining What Rights You Need

To shield you from an infringement suit, your license must authorize every type of use that you will be making of the licensed work. Consequently, you need to determine how you will be using the work and what rights you need before you seek the license. A license is no protection for uses not authorized in the license.

> **Example:** *Web Publisher obtained a license to reproduce Photographer's photograph of the Golden Gate bridge in a Web site. Although the license did not authorize Publisher to alter the photograph, Publisher manipulated the image to eliminate cars and pedestrians and create an uncluttered image of the bridge. If Photographer sued Publisher for unauthorized exercise of the modification right, Publisher's license would be no defense.*

Using a licensed work in ways not authorized in the license may be material breach of the license agreement. If it is, the licensor can terminate the license. In the previous example, Developer's alteration of the photograph is probably a material breach of Developer's license agreement with Photographer. If Photographer terminates the license, Developer will no longer have even the right granted to Developer in the license.

# Other Intellectual Property Laws

While copyright law is the most important intellectual property law for Internet users, you need to know enough about patent, trademark, and trade secrets law to avoid infringing intellectual property rights owned by others and to be able to take advantage of the protection these laws provide.

## Patent Law

Patent law protects inventions and processes ("utility" patents) and ornamental designs ("design" patents). Inventions and processes protected by utility patents can be electrical, mechanical, or chemical in nature. Internet-related works protectible by utility patents include communications protocols, data compression techniques, interfaces, encryption techniques, online payment systems, and information processing and retrieval technologies. Examples of works protected by design patents are a design for the sole of running shoes, a design for sterling silver tableware, and a design for a water fountain.

## Obtaining Patent Protection

There are strict requirements for the grant of utility patents and design patents. To qualify for a utility patent, an invention must be new, useful, and "nonobvious." To meet the novelty requirement, the invention must not have been known or used by others in this country before the applicant invented it, and it also must not have been patented or described in a printed publication in the U.S. or a foreign country before the applicant invented it. The policy behind the novelty requirement is that a patent is issued in exchange for the inventor's disclosure to the public of the details of his invention. If the inventor's work is not novel, the inventor is not adding to the public knowledge, so the inventor should not be granted a patent.

To meet the nonobviousness requirement, the invention must be sufficiently different from existing technology and knowledge so that, at the time the invention was made, the invention as a whole would not have been obvious to a person having ordinary skill in that field. The policy behind this requirement is that patents should only be granted for real advances, not for mere technical tinkering or modifications of existing inventions.

It is difficult to obtain a utility patent. Even if the invention or process meets the requirements of novelty, utility, and nonobviousness, a patent will not be granted if the invention was patented or described in a printed publication in the U.S. or a foreign country more than one year before the application date, or if the invention was in public use or on sale in the U.S. for more than one year before the application date.

## Scope of Protection

A patent owner has the right to exclude others from importing, making, using, or selling the patented invention or design in the United States during the term of the patent. Anyone who imports, makes, uses, or sells a patented invention or design within the United States during the term of the patent without permission from the patent owner is an infringer—even if he or she did not copy the patented invention or design or even know about it.

> **Example:** *Developer's staff members, working on their own, developed a software program for manipulating images in Developer's multimedia works. Although Developer's staff didn't know it, Inventor has a patent on that method of image manipulation. Developer's use of the software program infringes Inventor's patent.*

Utility patents filed before June 8, 1995 were granted for a period of 17 years and later were extended for the greater of 17 years after issuance or 20 years after filing. All utility patents filed on or after June 8, 1995 have a term of 20 years from filing, but this term may be extended under certain circumstances. Design patents are granted for a period of 14 years. Once the patent on an invention or design has expired, anyone is free to make, use, or sell the invention or design.

## Trademark Law

Trademarks and service marks are words, names, symbols, or devices used by manufacturers of goods and providers of services to identify their goods and services, and to distinguish their goods and services from goods manufactured and sold by others.

> **Example:** *The trademark* Quicken *is used by Intuit Inc. to identify Intuit's personal finance software and distinguish that software from other vendors' software.*

For trademarks used in commerce, federal trademark protection is available under the federal trademark statute, the Lanham Act. Many states have trademark registration statutes that resemble the Lanham Act, and all states protect unregistered trademarks under the common law (nonstatutory law) of trademarks.

## Availability of Protection

Trademark protection is available for words, names, symbols, or devices that are capable of distinguishing the owner's goods or services from the goods or services of others. A trademark that merely describes a class of goods rather than distinguishing the trademark owner's goods from goods provided by others is not protectible.

**Example:** *The word "corn flakes" is not protectible as a trademark for cereal because that term describes a type of cereal that is sold by a number of cereal manufacturers rather than distinguishing one cereal manufacturer's goods.*

A trademark that so resembles a trademark already in use in the U.S. as to be likely to cause confusion or mistake is not protectible. In addition, trademarks that are "descriptive" of the functions, quality, or character of the goods or services have special requirements before they will be protected.

## Obtaining Protection

The most effective trademark protection is obtained by filing a trademark registration application in the Patent and Trademark Office. Federal law also protects unregistered trademarks, but such protection is limited to the geographic area in which the mark is actually being used. State trademark protection under common law is obtained simply by adopting a trademark and using it in connection with goods or services. This protection is limited to the geographic area in which the trademark is actually being used. State statutory protection is obtained by filing an application with the state trademark office.

## Scope of Protection

Trademark law in general, whether federal or state, protects a trademark owner's commercial identity (goodwill, reputation, and investment in advertising) by giving the trademark owner the exclusive right to use the trademark on the type of goods or services for which the owner is using the trademark. Any person who uses a trademark in connection with goods or services in a way that is likely to cause confusion is an infringer. Trademark owners can obtain injunctions against the confusing use of their trademarks by others, and they can collect damages for infringement.

**Example:** *Small Multimedia Company is selling a line of interactive training works under the trademark* Personal Tutor. *If Giant Multimedia Company starts selling interactive training works under the trademark* Personal Tutor, *purchasers may think that Giant's works come from the same source as Small Multimedia's works. Giant is infringing Small's trademark.*

## Using Third-Party Trademarks

You should be careful to avoid using or showing other companies' trademarks on your Web site or in your online products without the owners' permission. A trademark owner may object to being associated with your company or your products.

In naming your own products, choose trademarks that do not infringe another company's trademark or trade name.

The relationship between trademarks and domain names is discussed in Form 12.

## Trade Secret Law

A trade secret is information of any sort that is valuable to its owner, not generally known, and that has been kept secret by the owner. Trade secrets are generally protected only under state law. Although a trade secret need not be unique in the patent law sense, information that is generally known is not protected under trade secrets law. Patent applicants generally rely on trade secret law to protect their inventions while the patent applications are pending. Inventions and processes that are not patentable can be protected under trade secret law.

The following types of technical and business information are examples of material that can be protected by trade secret law: customer lists, instructional methods, manufacturing processes, and methods of developing software.

### Obtaining Protection

Trade secret protection attaches automatically when information of value to the owner is kept secret by the owner.

A trade secret owner has the right to keep others from misappropriating and using the trade secret. Sometimes the misappropriation is a result of industrial espionage. Many trade secret cases involve people who have taken their former employers' trade secrets for use in new businesses or for new employers.

Trade secret owners have recourse only against misappropriation. Discovery of protected information through independent research or reverse engineering (taking a product apart to see how it works) is not misappropriation.

Trade secret protection endures so long as the requirements for protection—generally, value to the owner and secrecy—continue to be met. The protection is lost if the owner fails to take reasonable steps to keep the information secret. Measures to maintain secrecy include such steps as: marking documents as confidential, restricting employees' and outsiders' access to materials, and requiring employees and independent contractors to sign confidentiality agreements. Several of the forms in this book contain confidentiality provisions.

## Privacy And Defamation Law

In this section, we'll discuss the privacy and publicity laws, what restrictions privacy law puts on employer monitoring of employee email and Internet use, and defamation law.

## Privacy and Publicity

Most states in the United States recognize that individuals have a right of privacy. The right of privacy gives an individual a legal claim against someone who intrudes on the individual's physical solitude or seclusion, and against those who publicly disclose private facts. Remedies for invasion of privacy include injunctions against continued intrusion and damages for mental distress.

A related right, the right of publicity, gives the individual the right to control his name, face, image, signature, or voice for commercial purposes. Almost half the states in the United States recognize that individuals have a right of publicity.

> **Example:** *Web Developer took a picture of actor Clint Eastwood standing on a street corner in Carmel. Developer used the picture on Developer's marketing Web site. Unless Eastwood gave Developer permission to use Eastwood's image, Developer's use of the image violated Eastwood's right of publicity (even though Developer, as "author" of the photo, owned the copyright in the photo).*

You can avoid violating privacy/publicity rights by getting releases from individuals before using text, photographs, or video clips that include those individuals' names, faces, images, or voices for commercial purposes. Some writers, photographers, and video producers routinely obtain releases, but don't assume that this is the case. In Forms 2 and 3, we remind you to consider whether releases are needed. A release is included in this book (Form 5).

Newspapers and news magazines have a "media use" privilege to publish names or images in connection with reporting a newsworthy event. The "media use" privilege has been held to apply to documentaries and other nonprint media, so presumably it applies to the Internet as well. Also, generally you do not need a release to use a photograph of an individual for noncommercial purposes—to illustrate a point in a factual article, for example. However, if you use the same photograph to sell a product, you do need a release. If you are uncertain about whether your use is commercial, you should obtain the release.

In some states, an individual's right of publicity terminates when the individual dies. In other states, the right passes to the heirs of the deceased original owner. Don't use the name, voice, face, or image of a deceased celebrity—Marilyn Monroe or Martin Luther King, Jr., for example—without checking applicable state law.

## Employer Monitoring of Employee Email

Generally, employer monitoring of employees' email and Internet use does not violate the employees' right to privacy if done for legitimate business purposes. The question is whether the employer's need to monitor outweighs the employee's reasonable expectation of privacy. Employers who engage in monitoring should make it clear to their employees, in a written policy such as this book's Internet Use Policy (see Form 9), that employees should not expect to be free from monitoring.

## Defamation Law

Defamation law (also known as libel law) protects an individual against the dissemination of falsehoods about that individual. To be actionable, the falsehood must injure his or her reputation or subject the individual to hatred, contempt, or ridicule. A public figure or official must prove that the publisher or broadcaster made the statement either knowing it was false or entertaining serious doubts about its truth. A private individual only has to prove that the publisher or broadcaster acted negligently in failing to ascertain that the statement was false. The higher burden for public figures and officials flows from the First Amendment.

Here are some tips for avoiding the use of defamatory material:

- ■ *Original material.* If you plan to use any statements that could injure someone's reputation, make certain that you can prove that the statements are true. There is often a big difference between "knowing" that something is true and being able to prove that it is true. Journalists are taught to be particularly careful about statements concerning arrests and convictions and statements concerning professionals' qualifications and ethics.

- ■ *Photographs.* With digital editing software, it is now easy to edit and merge photographs. Avoid using an edited image that falsely associates an individual with controversial or unsavory events, places, or people. Using an altered image that puts a person in a "false light"—for example, a photograph created by merging a photograph of an elected official with a photograph of a Mafia figure—will expose you to liability for both libel and breach of privacy.

- ■ *Licensed material.* If licensed materials include potentially libelous material, don't use the material. If you use it, even though the material didn't originate with you, you could have liability for libel. We remind you about defamation law in Forms 2 and 3.

Corporations can recover damages for defamation. Many executives are zealous about protecting their corporation's reputation. If you make statements that might damage a corporation's reputation, make sure the statements are true.

An employer can be liable for defamatory statements made by employees within the scope of the employment. An employer's Internet Use Policy (see Form 9) should remind employees that they should not post defamatory material on the Internet or company intranet.

Whether system operators, online service providers, Internet access providers, and Chat Room providers should be held liable when defamatory content is posted by users has been debated. In one case, Prodigy was held liable as a publisher for allegedly defamatory statements posted by an unknown Prodigy subscriber on Prodigy's financial bulletin board. The plaintiff later withdrew the suit in exchange for a statement that Prodigy was sorry that the messages had been posted. Legislation enacted by Congress as part of the Communications Decency Act appears to resolve the issue for service providers by stating that "[n]o provider or user of an interactive computer service shall be treated as the pubisher or speaker of any information provided by another information content provider." Nonetheless, if you post user submissions on your Web site, your rules for users should include a prohibition against posting defamatory material (see Form 4 and 8).

## Contracts Law

A contract is a legally enforceable agreement between two or more parties. The core of most contracts is a set of mutual promises (in legal terminology, "consideration"). The promises made by the parties define the rights and obligations of the parties.

Contracts are enforceable in the courts. If one party meets its contractual obligations and the other party doesn't ("breaches the contract"), the nonbreaching party is entitled to receive relief through the courts.

Generally, the remedy for breach of contract is money damages that will put the nonbreaching party in the position it would have enjoyed if the contract had been performed. Under special circumstances, a court will order the breaching party to perform its contractual obligations.

In this country and most others, businesses have significant flexibility in setting the terms of their contracts. Contracts are, in a sense, private law created by the agreement of the parties. The rights and obligations of the parties are determined by the contract's terms, subject to limits imposed by relevant statutes.

Corporations have the power to enter into contracts. They make contracts through the acts of their agents, officers, and employees. Whether a particular employee has the power to bind the corporation to a contract is determined by an area of law called agency law or corporate law. If you doubt whether an individual with whom you are dealing has authority to enter into a contract with you, insist that the contract be reviewed and signed by the corporation's president.

A corporation has a separate legal existence from its founders, officers, and employees. Generally, the individuals associated with a corporation are not themselves responsible for the corporation's debts or liabilities, including liability for breach of contract.

### Offer and Acceptance

A contract is formed when one party (the "offeror") makes an offer which is accepted by the other party (the "offeree"). An offer—a proposal to form a contract—can be as simple as the words, "I'll wash your car for you for $15." An acceptance—the offeree's assent to the terms of the offer—can be as simple as, "You've got a deal." Sometimes acceptance can be shown by conduct rather than by words. It seems logical that clicking on a "Yes, I want it" icon on a Web site's order screen can signify acceptance, as can sending an email. However, there are no cases yet on electronic contract formation, so this issues has not been decided.

## Sales Law

In every state except Louisiana, a statute known as Article Two of the Uniform Commercial Code (UCC) applies to all contracts for the sale of goods.

In those states that have adopted Article Two, the rules of Article Two displace general contract law for all transactions in goods. Goods are defined as "all things (including specially manufactured goods) which are movable." Although Article Two currently does not apply to copyright licensing and contracts for services, many courts apply Article Two's provisions by analogy in disputes involving these kinds of contracts.

Ironically, Article Two of the UCC is not entirely uniform from state to state. California's version, for example, differs slightly from New York's version.

In international transactions, Article Two may be superseded by the United Nations Convention on the International Sale of Goods. This Convention applies to a transaction if both parties are located in countries that have joined the Convention, unless the parties have agreed that the Convention will not apply. The United States belongs to the Convention, as do many important commercial nations.

Some of Article Two's provisions apply only to "merchants." A merchant is defined in Article Two as "a person who deals in goods of the kind or otherwise by his occupation holds himself out as having knowledge or skill peculiar to the practices or goods involved in the transaction.". If you are selling goods on the Internet, you are probably a merchant for those goods.

## Important Provisions of Article Two

Article Two governs the substantive rights of the parties to a transaction. Freedom of contract is the guiding principle of Article Two: The parties to a business transaction may, by agreement, modify most of Article Two's rules.

## The Writing Requirement

According to Article Two, a contract for the sale of goods for $500 or more is not enforceable "unless there is some writing sufficient to indicate that a contract for sale has been made between the parties" and it is signed by the party against whom enforcement is sought (there are some exceptions). This provision doesn't require you to use a formal written contract. All you need from the buyer is a signed writing "sufficient to indicate that a contract for sale has been made." A writing is "sufficient" if it states the quantity term correctly. A writing is "signed" if it includes "any symbol executed or adopted by a party with present intention to authenticate a writing."

Presumably, for online sales the writing requirement is met if you have a reproducible record of the terms of the agreement and a record of the user's response stored in the computer's memory. A record of a buyer's emailed response to your offer should also satisfy the requirement, so long as it is clear that the buyer intended to form a contract.

In online ordering, it seems logical that the buyer's filling in of his or her name on the order form should count as a signature. In an email, the buyer's email symbol on the "from" line may count as a signature.

A few states—California, Minnesota, Texas, Utah, and Washington—have passed laws to make it clear that a "digital signature" satisfies the "signed writing" requirement. A digital signature is a piece of data added to a communication to indicate that a certain person agreed to or authorized the contents of the communication. Digital signature technology allows the recipient to verify the source and the integrity of the communication.

## Warranties

Article Two provides for four types of warranties in connection with the sale of goods:

- ■ Implied warranty of merchantability.
- ■ Implied warranty of fitness for particular purpose.
- ■ Implied warranties of title and noninfringement.
- ■ Express warranty.

For the three types of implied warranties, you should be aware that you may be making these warranties every time you sell your product unless you take appropriate steps to exclude the warranties.

## Implied Warranty of Merchantability

When a merchant (defined earlier in this chapter) sells goods, a warranty that the goods are "merchantable" is implied in the contract unless that warranty is excluded. To be merchantable, goods must "pass without objection in the trade" and be "fit for the ordinary purposes for which such goods are used."

> **Example:** *Big Company purchased a spreadsheet program that does not add correctly. The program is not "merchantable" because it is not fit for the ordinary purposes for which spreadsheets are used. Unless the seller excluded the implied warranty of merchantability for the sale, the seller gave Big Company an implied warranty that the program was merchantable. The seller is liable to Big Company for breaching the implied warranty of merchantability.*

To avoid disputes over whether goods are merchantable, many manufacturers and sellers of goods exclude the warranty of merchantability. Article Two states that this warranty can be excluded only with language that mentions merchantability. If the exclusion is in writing (and it should be, for evidence purposes), the exclusion must be "conspicuous" (in a different typeface, type size, or color from the rest of the contract). This warranty also can be excluded by making it clear in the contract that the goods are sold "as is."

## Implied Warranty of Fitness

The "implied warranty of fitness for particular purpose" is made by a seller when two factors are present: (1) The seller has reason to know of a particular purpose for which the buyer requires the goods, and (2) the buyer relies on the seller's skill or judgment to select suitable goods. The implied warranty of fitness for particular purpose can be excluded through contract language that explicitly excludes this warranty or by selling products "as is."

## Implied Warranties of Title and Noninfringement

Unless excluded, each contract for the sale of goods also includes a warranty by the seller that the seller has the right to transfer title in the goods and that the buyer will get good title. The warranty of title can be excluded only by specific language or by circumstances that give the buyer reason to know that the person selling does not claim full title. Unless otherwise agreed, a "merchant" warrants that the goods sold do not infringe third parties' intellectual property rights.

## Disclaiming Warranties

Many manufacturers and sellers of consumer products disclaim all of Article Two's implied warranties. Instead, they warrant only that the product will, for a limited period of time, be free from defects in materials and craftsmanship under normal use and service.

State consumer protection laws and the Magnuson-Moss Warranty Act must be considered in drafting warranty language. The Magnuson-Moss Warranty Act is a federal statute that applies to consumer products manufactured after July 4, 1975. The statute defines "consumer product" as "any tangible personal property that is distributed in commerce and that is normally used for personal, family, or household purposes."

The purpose is of the statute is to make warranties on consumer products more understandable and enforceable. It prohibits disclaiming or modifying the Article Two implied warranties in the sale of a consumer product if a written warranty is given.

## Express Warranties

A seller can create express warranties by making statements of fact or promises to the buyer, by a description of the goods, or by display of a sample or model. An express warranty can be created—in the physical world or in the online world—without using formal words such as "warranty" or "guarantee." All that is necessary is that the statements, description, or sample become part of the "basis of the bargain." To avoid making express warranties that you don't mean to make, you must be careful about what you say—and what your marketing representatives say—in marketing your product or service.

## Remedies

According to Article Two, a buyer can obtain actual damages along with "incidental damages" and "consequential damages" from a seller who breaches a contract. Incidental damages are those resulting from the seller's breach of contract, such as expenses incurred in inspecting and transporting rejected goods and obtaining substitute goods. Consequential damages include any loss that could not reasonably be prevented by the buyer that resulted from the buyer's requirements and needs that the seller knew about (or had reason to know about). Consequential damages also include damages for injury to person or property resulting from a breach of warranty.

Article Two states that a contract may provide for remedies "in addition to or in substitution for those provided in this Article and may limit or alter the measure of damages recoverable under this Article." Unless the contract remedy is the buyer's exclusive remedy, the buyer can choose from the Article Two remedies or the contractual remedy. Many manufacturers and sellers of products limit the buyer's remedy to repair of the defect in the product, replacement of the product, or refund of the purchase price.

Most product manufacturers and sellers try to exclude consequential damages because such liability exposes a seller to a risk of having to pay damages far in excess of the product's price. Consequential damages may be limited or excluded unless the limitation or exclusion is "unconscionable." The term "unconscionable" is not defined in Article Two, but many courts have used the definition created by one of the federal appellate courts: "Unconscionability has generally been recognized to include an absence of meaningful choice on the part of one of the parties together with contract terms which are unreasonably favorable to the other party." In the case of consumer goods, limitation of consequential damages for personal injury is assumed to be unconscionable.

If a seller excludes consequential damages or otherwise contractually limits remedies and then "circumstances cause the... remedy to fail of its essential purpose" (that is, leave the buyer with no real remedy), all of Article Two's normal remedies are available to the buyer, possibly even consequential damages.

In one case involving a contractual limitation on damages, the buyer, a hospital, had paid the seller, the software supplier Electronic Data Systems Corporation, more than $2 million for software systems. The software systems were so defective the hospital could not use them. The contract provision limited the hospital's damages to $4,000, the amount of the average monthly invoice for the transaction. The court found that because the hospital had paid more than $2 million for unusable software systems, the $4,000 limit on damages failed to provide the hospital with an adequate remedy and thus "failed of its essential purpose."

To avoid such a determination, many manufacturers and sellers who limit the customer's remedy to repair or replacement also promise that they will refund the purchase price if the product cannot be repaired or replaced. The refund promise is a "backup" remedy.

## Clickwraps and Shrinkwraps

Many companies are beginning to use "clickwrap" agreements to define the terms and conditions of transactions, to disclaim implied warranties of merchantability and fitness, and to limit liability.

Software sellers have long used "shrinkwrap" agreements on product packaging for these purposes. Whether shrinkwraps are enforceable is uncertain (some people take the position that they are unenforceable "contracts of adhesion" because consumers cannot really bargain with the seller). If the purchaser does not have the opportunity to review the terms of the shrinkwrap prior to purchase, enforceability is particularly questionable.

Under a proposed revision to the UCC, shrinkwraps and clickwraps will be enforceable only if the user actively manifests assent after having had an opportunity to review the terms. A user has an "opportunity to review" the license terms if the license is available before the user gets access, such that the user's attention is called to the terms or provided in a conspicuous manner during the normal first use of the work. A user manifests assent if, having had an opportunity to review a license that states what conduct would constitute acceptance and having had the opportunity not to take such action, he or she engages in such conduct. Forms 4, 8, and 10 include tips on how to provide for an "opportunity to review" and the manifestation of assent in online transactions.

# FORM 1

# Development and Transfer Agreement

## (For Copyrighted Material)

IF YOU ARE PLANNING TO USE the services of a freelancer or nonemployee to create graphics, photographs, text, or music for your Web site, you will need Form 1 to avoid lawsuits. If you plan to use existing material, use Forms 2 or 3 (content licenses) instead.

You should also use Form 1 if you are a graphic designer, photographer, writer, or musician who creates content for others' Web sites.

When content for a Web site is created by a freelancer (also known as an independent contractor) for a client, a contract is important for two reasons: (1) to clarify and document the two parties' understanding about their respective obligations and rights; (2) to deal with the issue of who will own the copyright in the material created by the freelancer. Under current U.S. law, when a hiring party and an independent contractor fail to address the issue of who will own the copyright in the material created by the contractor, the contractor owns the copyright.

**Cross-References**

For a discussion of the applicable laws for Form 1, see the following sections in the Overview: Copyright Law, Copyright Ownership, Copyright Licenses, Other Intellectual Property Laws, and Contracts Law.

This form assumes that the project is a simple one that does not include detailed milestones (defined phases for the Contractor's contractual obligations). This form refers to the hiring party as "Client" and to the freelancer as "Contractor." The services which Contractor agrees to perform are the "Project," and the material created by Contractor during the Project is the "Work Product."

## Checklist of Issues

1. What is the Contractor being hired to do or create (Section 1)? Vagueness in the contract can camouflage misunderstanding that will come to light when the Contractor delivers the finished work, so be as specific as possible. Client should include a detailed statement of what the Contractor is to deliver, because this statement will help both parties make certain that they agree on what the Contractor is promising.
2. What compensation will Client pay Contractor, and when is payment due (Section 2.1)? The agreement assumes a one-time payment, but there are other options—for example, an annual fee for each year the Work Product is used by Client, or partial payment each time the Contractor completes a milestone.
3. Who will be responsible for expenses—for example, materials costs and processing fees (Section 2.2)?
4. How will the Client decide that the Work Product is what it wanted? The acceptance provision in Section 2.2 suggests one approach to this problem.
5. Will Contractor be receiving confidential information from Client? If so, include a confidentiality provision such as Section 4.2.
6. Who will own the copyright in the Work Product? By addressing this issue in the written agreement, the parties will eliminate future legal disputes over ownership. Section 5.2 provides that Contractor assigns all rights in the Work Product to Client. If Contractor is to retain ownership, Section 5.2 must be modified to make that clear and to define what rights Client will have to use the Work Product. Technically, if the contract says nothing about copyright ownership, Contractor automatically owns the copyright in the work (and Client has only an implied license of uncertain scope to use the Work Product). Although many people think that ordering and paying for material automatically means that they will own the copyright, they are wrong. The contract should address the copyright ownership issue in order to eliminate misunderstandings.
7. What warranties will be given by Contractor (Section 7)?

8. What remedy will Client have if the Work Product is not as warranted? Section 8 is a typical indemnification provision.

## Negotiating Tips: Client

■ *Copyright Ownership.* Generally, you should try to obtain ownership of copyrights in material created for you by independent contractors. If you do so, you will then have all the copyright owner's exclusive rights in the material—including the right to use the material in later projects and different media as well as the right to modify the material.

However, you should understand that in certain situations Contractor may resist giving you outright copyright ownership. If Contractor is to retain copyright ownership of the entire Work Product, make certain that the contract gives you the right to use the Work Product in every way and every media that you believe will be necessary, now and in the future. You will find helpful language in Forms 2 and 3.

If you and Contractor cannot agree on the allocation of copyright ownership, you may be able to compromise by letting Contractor retain copyright ownership of particular components of the Project—such as a particular graphic—while giving you copyright ownership of everything else (see Section 5.3).

■ *Standard Forms.* Professionals in many fields have professional associations that have developed and distributed standard forms for use by their members. If Contractor insists on using a standard form, read it carefully, particularly the provisions relating to copyright ownership.

■ *Warranties and Indemnities.* You should try to get warranties and an indemnity from Contractor (see Sections 7 and 8). The warranties are designed to ensure two things: (1) that Contractor worked alone in developing the Work Product (so that Contractor can assign you ownership of the copyright in the Work Product or license you rights to the Work Product), and (2) that Contractor did not incorporate third-party material into the Work Product. If the Work Product contains material that infringes a third party's copyright, the use of such material on your Web site will make you liable for infringement of the third party's copyright, even if you were not aware of the infringement. These provisions are designed to give you legal recourse against a Contractor who uses material owned by others.

■ *Services of an Individual.* If you enter into a contract with a Contractor which is a corporation and expect to get the services of particular individuals employed by the corporation, the contract should state that the work can be done only by the named individuals. Otherwise, the corporation will be free to use any of its employees to do the job.

## Negotiating Tips: Contractor

■ *Deadlines.* You should make certain that the deadline (in Section 1) is realistic. Serious delay on your part can be grounds for termination by the Client. If Client is entitled to terminate the contract because of your failure to deliver the project on time, you may have to absorb the costs that went into the project before the termination. Normally, Client will have no obligation to reimburse you for those costs.

■ *Acceptance Clause.* For your protection, the proposal and contract should provide a procedure and a deadline for Client objections to the delivered Work Product (see Section 2.2). You need to know that after a certain period of time passes, it will be too late for the Client to say, "I won't accept this. Do it again."

■ *Copyright Ownership.* If you agree to assign the copyright in the Work Product to Client, you will not be able to use that material in other projects or modify it for other projects. Once you assign the copyright, Client will have the copyright owner's exclusive rights to reproduce the Work Product, distribute it, publicly perform it, publicly display it, and modify it for use in derivative works. However, you will still be able to re-use ideas that you used in the Work Product.

If you are creating material to fill Client's special needs, you may not object to giving Client ownership of the copyright (particularly if Client is willing to pay a higher fee for an assignment of all rights). You may, however, want to retain ownership of components—for example, certain graphics—that you created for the Work Product, or at least reserve the right to use the components in future projects. You can use Section 5.3 to do that. Unless you retain copyright ownership of the components or get a license from Client to re-use them, your use of the components in future projects will infringe Client's copyright.

If the copyright in the Work Product is to be owned by Client, you may want to include a clause in the contract authorizing you to make copies of the Work Product to show to future clients. Or you may want the right to make limited use of the Work Product or components of the Work Product in other projects. You can use Exhibit B, "Contractor's License to Use the Work Product," to do that. You will find helpful language for filling out Exhibit B in Forms 2 and 3.

■ *Warranties and Indemnity.* Client will probably insist that the contract include representations and warranties from you (see Sections 7 and 8). Warranty clauses typically include an indemnity provision in which the warrantor promises to defend, indemnify, and hold the other party harmless for the breach of any of the warranties (in other words, pay all costs, including attorneys' fees, arising out of the breach of the warranties). Clients have good reason for asking for warranties and indemnities: If you infringe any third-party copyrights in creating the Work Product, Client will also violate those rights by using the Work Product (even though innocent of intent to infringe). If the warranty and indemnity provisions make you nervous, try to negotiate for a dollar limit for your indemnity—for example, no more than your total Project compensation.

- ***Credit.*** You may want to try to get Client to agree to include a credit for you when using the Work Product. If Client agrees to a credit, specify in the contract how your credit should read, where it should be placed, and at what point Client will be free to delete the credit (for example, after substantial changes have been made to the Work Product). If you have a Web site, you may want the credit to include a link to your Web site.

# COPYRIGHT DEVELOPMENT AND TRANSFER AGREEMENT

THIS AGREEMENT ("Agreement") is entered into by and between _____ (the "Client") _____ and _____(the "Contractor") on the _____(the "Effective Date").

NOW, THEREFORE, in consideration of the promises and mutual covenants and agreements set forth herein, the parties agree as follows:

1. Engagement of Services. Contractor agrees to perform services for Client as follows:_____
   ("Project"). Contractor may not subcontract or otherwise delegate its obligations under this Agreement without Client's prior written consent. Contractor agrees to perform the services in a professional manner and to complete the Project by _____.

2. Compensation.

   2.1 Fees and Approved Expenses. Client will pay Contractor the fee of _____ for services rendered by Contractor pursuant to this Agreement. Contractor will not be reimbursed for any expenses incurred in connection with the performance of services under this Agreement, unless those expenses are approved in advance and in writing by Client or listed in Exhibit A as Reimbursable Expenses.

   2.2 Payment Due. Client will review the Work Product within _____ (_____) days after receiving it from Contractor to ensure that it meets the Project requirements stated in Section 1. If Client does not give written notice of rejection to Contractor within that time period (describing the reasons for the rejection in reasonable detail), the Work Product will be deemed to be accepted. Client will pay Contractor for services and will reimburse Contractor for previously approved expenses within _____ (____) days after acceptance.

3. Independent Contractor Relationship. Contractor and Client understand, acknowledge, and agree that Contractor's relationship with Client will be that of an independent contractor and nothing in this Agreement is intended to or should be construed to create a partnership, joint venture, or employment relationship.

4. Trade Secrets and Confidential Information

   4.1 Third-Party Information. Contractor represents that his performance of all of the terms of this Agreement does not and will not breach any agreement to keep in confidence proprietary information, knowledge or data of a third party and Contractor will not disclose to Client, or induce Client to use, any confidential or proprietary information belonging to third parties unless such use or disclosure is authorized in writing by such owners.

   4.2 Confidential Information. Contractor agrees during the term of this Agreement and thereafter to take all steps reasonably necessary to hold in trust and confidence information which he knows or has reason to know is considered confidential by Client ("Confidential Information"). Contractor agrees to use the Confidential Information solely to perform the Project hereunder. Confidential Information includes, but is not limited to, technical and business information relating to Client's inventions or products, research and development, manufacturing and engineering processes, and future business plans. Contractor's obligations with respect to the Confidential Information also extend to any third party's proprietary or confidential information disclosed to Contractor in the course of providing services to Client. This obligation shall not extend to any information which becomes generally known to the public without breach of this Agreement. This obligation shall survive the termination of this Agreement.

5. Ownership of Work Product.

5.1 Definition. "Work Product" means the works of authorship conceived or developed by Contractor while performing the Project services.

5.2 Assignment. Contractor hereby irrevocably assigns, conveys and otherwise transfers to Client, and its respective successors and assigns, all rights, title and interests worldwide in and to the Work Product and all copyrights, contract and licensing rights, and claims and causes of action of any kind with respect to any of the foregoing, whether now known or hereafter to become known (except as stated otherwise in Section 5.3). In the event Contractor has any rights in and to the Work Product that cannot be assigned to Client, Contractor hereby unconditionally and irrevocably waives the enforcement of all such rights, and all claims and causes of action of any kind with respect to any of the foregoing against Client, its distributors and customers, whether now known or hereafter to become known and agrees, at the request and expense of Client and its respective successors and assigns, to consent to and join in any action to enforce such rights and to procure a waiver of such rights from the holders of such rights. In the event Contractor has any rights in and to the Work Product that cannot be assigned to Client and cannot be waived, Contractor hereby grants to Client, and its respective successors and assigns, an exclusive, worldwide, royalty-free license during the term of the rights to reproduce, distribute, modify, publicly perform and publicly display, with the right to sublicense through multiple tiers of sublicensees, and the right to assign such rights in and to the Work Product including, without limitation, the right to use in any way whatsoever the Work Product. Contractor retains no rights to use the Work Product except as stated in Exhibit B and agrees not to challenge the validity of the copyright ownership by Client in the Work Product.

5.3. Ownership of Components. Contractor will retain copyright ownership of the following components: _____ ("Retained Components"). However, Contractor grants to Client a royalty-free, worldwide, perpetual, irrevocable, nonexclusive license, with the right to sublicense through multiple tiers of sublicensees, to reproduce, distribute, modify, publicly perform and publicly display the Retained Components on any Web site operated by or for Client and in marketing material.

5.4 Power of Attorney. Contractor agrees to assist Client in any reasonable manner to obtain and enforce for Client's benefit copyrights covering the Work Product in any and all countries. Contractor agrees to execute, when requested, copyright, or similar applications and assignments to Client, and any other lawful documents deemed necessary by Client to carry out the purpose of this Agreement. Contractor further agrees that the obligations and undertaking stated in this Section 5.4 will continue beyond the termination of Contractor's service to Client. If called upon to render assistance under this Section 5.4, Contractor will be entitled to a fair and reasonable fee in addition to reimbursement of authorized expenses incurred at the prior written request of Client. In the event that Client is unable for any reason whatsoever to secure Contractor's signature to any lawful and necessary document required to apply for or execute any patent, copyright or other applications with respect to any Work Product, Contractor hereby irrevocably designates and appoints Client and its duly authorized officers and agents as his agents and attorneys-in-fact to act for and in his behalf and instead of Contractor, to execute and file any such application and to do all other lawfully permitted acts to further the prosecution and issuance of copyrights or other similar rights thereon with the same legal force and effect as if executed by Contractor.

6. Return of Client's Property. Contractor acknowledges that Client's sole and exclusive property includes all documents, such as drawings, manuals, notebooks, reports, sketches, records, computer programs, employee lists, customer lists and the like in his custody or possession, whether delivered to Contractor by Client or made by Contractor in the performance of services under this Agreement, relating to the business activities of Client or its customers or suppliers and containing any information or data whatsoever, whether or not Confidential Information. Contractor agrees to deliver promptly all of Client's property and all copies of Client's property in Contractor's possession to Client at any time upon Client's request.

7. Warranties. Contractor represents and warrants that:

(a) The Work Product was created solely by him, his full-time employees during the course of their employment, or independent contractors who assigned all right, title and interest worldwide in their work to Contractor.

(b) Contractor is the owner of all right, title and interest in the tangible forms of the Work Product and all intellectual property rights protecting them. The Work Product and the intellectual property rights protecting them are free and clear of all encumbrances, including, without limitation, security interests, licenses, liens, charges or other restrictions;

(c) Contractor has maintained the Work Product in confidence.

(d) The use, reproduction, distribution, or modification of the Work Product does not and will not violate the rights of any third parties in the Work Product including, but not limited to, copyrights, trade secrets, trademarks, publicity and privacy.

(e) The Work Product is not in the public domain.

(f) Contractor has full power and authority to make and enter into this Agreement.

8. Indemnification. Contractor agrees to defend, indemnify, and hold harmless Client, their officers, directors, sublicensees, employees and agents, from and against any claims, actions or demands, including without limitation reasonable legal and accounting fees, alleging or resulting from the breach of the warranties in Section 7. Client shall provide notice to Contractor promptly of any such claim, suit, or proceeding and shall assist Contractor, at Contractor's expense, in defending any such claim, suit or proceeding.

9. General Provisions. This Agreement will be governed by and construed in accordance with the laws of the United States and the State of _____ as applied to agreements entered into and to be performed entirely within that state between residents of that state. This Agreement, including any Exhibits to this Agreement, constitutes the entire agreement between the parties relating to this subject matter and supersedes all prior or simultaneous representations, discussions, negotiations, and agreements, whether written or oral. The Agreement may not be modified except by written instrument signed by both parties. No term or provision hereof will be considered waived by either party, and no breach excused by either party, unless such waiver or consent is in writing signed on behalf of the party against whom the waiver is asserted. No consent by either party to, or waiver of, a breach by either party, whether express or implied, will constitute a consent to, waiver of, or excuse of any other, different, or subsequent breach by either party. Contractor may not assign its rights or obligations arising under this Agreement without Client's prior written consent. Client may assign its rights and obligations under this Agreement. This Agreement will be for the benefit of Client's successors and assigns, and will be binding on Contractor's heirs, legal representatives and permitted assignees. If any dispute arises between the parties with respect to the matters covered by this Agreement which leads to a proceeding to resolve such dispute, the prevailing party in such proceeding shall be entitled to receive its reasonable attorneys' fees, expert witness fees and out-of-pocket costs incurred in connection with such proceeding, in addition to any other relief to which it may be entitled. All notices, requests and other communications required to be given under this Agreement must be in writing, and must be mailed by registered or certified mail, postage prepaid and return receipt requested, or delivered by hand to the party to whom such notice is required or permitted to be given. Any such notice will be considered to have been given when received, or if mailed, five (5) business days after it was mailed, as evidenced by the postmark. The mailing address for notice to either party will be the address shown on the signature page of this Agreement. Either party may change its mailing address by notice as provided by this Section. The following provisions shall survive termination of this Agreement: Sections 4, 5, 6, 7 and 8.

This Agreement is effective as of _____, 19____.

By: _____  By: _____

Typed name                      Typed name

Title                           Title

Address                         Address

**EXHIBIT A**
Reimbursable Expenses

**EXHIBIT B**
Contractor's License to Use the Work Product

# FORM 2

# Content License

## (Text)

FOUND SOME GREAT TEXT FOR YOUR WEB SITE, intranet, or online product? If so, you probably need this form. Although older text may be in the "public domain" and not protected by copyright, most text is protected by copyright law (even if it doesn't contain a copyright notice). Moreover, even if text is in the public domain in the United States, it may be protected by copyright in other countries. If you use copyrighted text without getting a license—permission from the copyright owner — you may find yourself facing a copyright infringement lawsuit.

You also need this form if you are a writer who has created text that other people want to use. While your oral grant of permission ("yes, you may use it") would be valid, by using this form you can be specific about what uses of your material you are permitting and for how long.

This form assumes that the text is being licensed for nonexclusive use. It also assumes that the text being licensed is already in existence. If a writer is being hired to create text for a Web site, use Form 1.

**Cross-References**

For a discussion of the applicable laws for Form 2, see the following sections in the Overview: Copyright Law, Copyright Ownership, Copyright Licenses, Privacy and Defamation Law, and Contracts Law.

This form refers to the copyright owner as "Licensor" and to the party receiving permission to use the text as "Licensee." The material being licensed is "the Work." The projects or products in which Licensee is permitted to use "the Work" is "the Project."

This form protects you from copyright infringement lawsuits. However, the use of text may lead to liability under other laws. For example, if the text invades the privacy of an individual or makes false and negative statements about someone, you may be liable for invasion of privacy, misappropriation of the individual's right of publicity, or defamation.

## Checklist Of Issues

1. What is being licensed (Section 1, "The Work")? To avoid later disputes, the parties should be as specific as possible. Here's an example of what should go in the blank in Section 1:

   "the text of Chapter 7 of the second edition of the book *Multimedia Law and Business Handbook.*"

   If the text being licensed is short, the parties could include a photocopy. If the copyright for the text has been registered with the Copyright Office, it may be identified by the title used in the registration certificate (for example, a book's title). If excerpts of a work are being licensed—not the whole work—the agreement should make that clear.

2. In what projects or products will Licensee be permitted to use the "Work" (Section 2, the "Project?") For example, is Licensee obtaining the right to use the material in Licensee's Web site or its intranet? In an online encyclopedia? In marketing material of any sort, including "print media" material?

   Be specific in filling out Section 2. Here's an example of what should go in the blank:

   "The Web site operated by or for Licensee at the URL www.newsite.com and marketing material in any media relating to such Web site."

3. What rights are being granted (Section 3)? As written, Section 3 provides for a broad grant of rights. If the Project includes a Web site, Section 3 gives Licensee the right to permit end users of the Web site to download one copy of the text for personal, noncommercial use. If the Project includes an internal network

(intranet), Section 3 gives Licensee's employees the right to copy the text for Licensee's internal business purposes.

4. Is the license exclusive or nonexclusive? Modify Section 3 if the license is to be exclusive.
5. Will Licensor get a credit? If so, how will it read (Section 4)?
6. What is the license fee (Section 5)? It could be a single one-time fee or an annual fee for each year Licensee uses the Work. The license fee does not have to be money. It could be products or services, publicity, or just a credit.
7. What is the term (duration) of the license (Section 6)? It can be perpetual or limited in duration.
8. What warranties is Licensor giving (Section 7)?
9. What remedy will Licensee have if the text is not as warranted (Section 8)?
10. Does the text use the names of actual individuals? If so, Licensee may need a privacy/publicity release in addition to a copyright license unless Licensor has already obtained one. Also, Licensee should consider whether the text is defamatory.
11. Does the text mention other companies' trademarks in a way which suggests an association with such companies? If so, Licensee may need permission from the trademark owners.

## Negotiating Tips: Licensee

- ***Time Requirements.*** Licensing is a slow process. You may find that some of the material you want to use is not available, and you may encounter unexpected delays. For example, using text on a Web site requires a worldwide license, and different parties may own rights to the text in different countries. In book publishing, the copyright is frequently assigned to other companies in foreign countries. The United States publisher may not be able to license worldwide rights. One selection of text used by IBM in its CD-ROM on Christopher Columbus required permission from more than five different parties.
- ***Alternatives.*** Don't plan your project around particular text unless you are confident that you can obtain a license to use it. The text may have already been licensed on an exclusive basis, or it may not be available at a reasonable price.
- ***Definition of "the Project."*** Pay careful attention to Section 2, the "Project." This license will give you the right to use the licensed text in specific endeavors, as defined in "the Project." If you use the material in a project that is outside the

definition of the Project, the license will not protect you. For example, if the license gives you the right to use the licensed text on your Web site and you use the text in print publications you sell to customers, your license will not protect you. Before you fill out Section 2, try to think of every way in which you might want to use the licensed text, now and in the future.

For example, you may wish to post the text on your company's intranet and distribute it by email. If so, you should describe the Project broadly as the "internal network operated by or for Licensee and its subsidiaries, including distribution by email or other electronic means to employees of Licensee and its subsidiaries as well as display and performance on such network of Licensee and its subsidiaries." This license includes the right for the employees of Licensee and its subsidiaries to copy the Work from the network for Licensee's internal business purposes.

■ *Grant of Rights.* The grant of rights (Section 3 ) in this form gives you broad rights to use the licensed text. If Licensor revises the grant or rights or substitutes his or her own version, read the rights grant carefully and make certain that it meets your needs. Generally, the use of text on a Web site requires only a license to the reproduction, distribution, and public display rights. However, you may need additional rights such as the right to modify the text. If you intend to use the text as a "voice-over" in a game, you will need a public performance right.

Section 3 provides if the Project includes a Web site, end users of your Web site may download the text for their own use. If Licensor insists on limiting "end user" downloading to downloading for personal, noncommercial use (as Section 3 provides), make sure your Web site terms and conditions contain this limitation.

■ *Warranties and Indemnity.* You should try to get warranties and an indemnity from Licensor to ensure that Licensor has sufficient rights to grant you the rights granted in Section 3. Sections 7 and 8 are typical warranty and indemnity provisions. These provisions are designed to give you legal recourse against a Licensor whose text includes material owned by others, or one who has already licensed the text on an exclusive basis to someone else. If a Licensor provides you with text that infringes a third party's copyright, the use of that material in your Web site, intranet, or online products will make you liable for infringement of the third party's copyright even if you were not aware of the infringement.

## Negotiating Tips: Licensor

■ *Definition of The "Project."* Get Licensee to be specific about how Licensee plans to use your text. You may not want your material used in Licensee's project, or you may not want to be associated with Licensee's products or services. If Licensee wants to define "the Project" broadly, remember that a license to use text in multiple projects or in a broadly defined, open-ended project generally should cost more than a license to use text in a single, narrowly defined project.

Make sure that the definition of the "Project" is not ambiguous. You and Licensee need to agree on what uses of your text you are authorizing, and Section 1 needs to clearly state that understanding. If you don't understand Licensee's terminology, get help (legal or technical). Don't sign a license without understanding what uses you are authorizing Licensee to make of your text.

■ *Grant of Rights.* The grant of rights stated in Section 3 may be broader than what you are willing to grant. If so, you need to modify this provision. For example, you may not want to grant Licensee the right to modify the text or you may want the right to approve modifications.

If Licensee wants a broad exclusive license, consider that you will be giving up the right to license the material to others, and charge a higher fee. Perhaps Licensee will be content with a short-duration exclusive license or with a narrow exclusive license—for example, the exclusive right to use the material for Web-based marketing directed at physicians.

Section 3 states that if the Project includes a Web site, end users of the Web site will have the right to download your text for their own use. You should make certain that such downloading is permitted only for the Web site users' personal, noncommercial use (so that you can obtain additional license revenue for commercial uses).

If you sell your text on a subscription basis and the license is for use of the text on Licensee's intranet, you may want to state that Licensee's use rights do not begin until several weeks after your publication date (to avoid having the electronic version compete with your print version). You also may want to require that Licensee not reduce the number of its current subscriptions.

■ *Warranties and Indemnity.* Licensee probably will insist that the contract include representations and warranties from you (see Sections 7 and 8). Warranty clauses typically include an indemnity provision in which Licensor promises to defend, indemnify, and hold Licensee harmless for the breach of any of the warranties (in other words, pay for all costs, including attorneys' fees, arising out of the breach of the warranties). Licensees have good reason for asking for warranties and indemnities: If the licensed text infringes any third-party copyrights, Licensee will also infringe those rights by using the text (even though innocent of intent to infringe). If the warranty and indemnity provisions make you nervous, try to negotiate for dollar limit for your exposure on the indemnity—for example, no more than the license fee.

The warranty provision includes a warranty that use of the licensed text will not violate the rights of publicity or privacy of any individual (Section 7(c)). If your text uses the names of an actual individual and you need a privacy release but do not have it (see the Overview), you should delete that provision and make it clear that Licensee has the responsibility to obtain any necessary releases.

■ *Credit.* You may want to try to get Licensee to agree to include a credit for you when using the text, as Section 4 provides (so that others who want to license your text will know how to find you). If Licensee agrees to a credit, specify in the contract how your credit should read and where it should be placed. If you have a Web site, you may want the credit to include a link to your Web site.

# TEXT LICENSE AGREEMENT

This agreement is made and entered into by and between ___ ("Licensor") and ___ ("Licensee") on the _____ (the "Effective Date").

NOW, THEREFORE, in consideration of the promises and mutual covenants and agreements set forth herein, the parties agree as follows:

1. DESCRIPTION OF WORK BEING LICENSED: _____
   _____ (the "Work").
2. DESCRIPTION OF PROJECTS OR PRODUCTS TO WHICH LICENSE APPLIES:
   _____ ("the Project").
3. GRANT OF RIGHTS: For good and valuable consideration, the receipt and sufficiency of which are hereby acknowledged, Licensor hereby grants to Licensee a nonexclusive license to reproduce, digitize, modify for editorial purposes for use on the Project (without destroying the integrity or meaning of the Work), publicly display, and distribute the Work as part of the Project and any advertising and promotion related to the Project. If the Project includes an internal network, this license includes the right of employees of Licensee and its subsidiaries to copy the work from the network for Licensee's internal business purposes. If the Project includes a Web site, this license includes the right to permit users of the Web site to reproduce one copy of the Work for their personal, noncommercial use, and Licensee shall so state in its Web site conditions of usage. This license shall not include the right to use the Work independently of the Project or advertising and promotion related thereto. The rights granted herein shall not confer in Licensor any rights of ownership in the Project, including, without limitation, the copyright thereto, all of which shall be and remain the exclusive property of Licensee, except that Licensor shall retain copyright in the Work.
4. CREDIT: In consideration of the rights granted to Licensee, and provided the Work is used in the Project, Licensee agrees to give Licensor credit in writing in the Project in substantially the following form: _____

   Any inadvertent failure to provide credit shall not be deemed a breach of this Agreement.
5. LICENSE FEE: In further consideration of the rights granted to Producer herein, Producer shall pay to Licensor the sum of $_____.
6. TERM. This license begins on ___ and ends on _____.
7. WARRANTIES. Licensor represents and warrants that:

   (a) the Work was created solely by him, his full-time employees during the course of their employment, or independent contractors who assigned all right, title and interest worldwide in their work to Licensor or Licensor has obtained sufficient rights to grant the license stated in Section 3;

   (b) Licensor is the owner of all right, title and interest in the tangible forms of the Work and all intellectual property rights protecting them or has the right to grant the license in Section 3. The Work and the intellectual property rights protecting them are free and clear of all encumbrances, including, without limitation, security interests, licenses, liens, charges or other restrictions which conflict with the license in Section 3;

(c) The use, public display, public performance, reproduction, distribution, or modification of the Work does not and will not violate the rights of any third parties in the Work including, but not limited to, copyrights, publicity and privacy;

(d) The Work is not in the public domain;

(e) Licensor has full power and authority to make and enter into this Agreement.

8. INDEMNIFICATION. Licensor agrees to defend, indemnify, and hold harmless Licensee and their officers, directors, employees and agents, from and against any claims, actions or demands, including without limitation reasonable legal and accounting fees, alleging or resulting from the breach of the warranties in Section 7. Licensee shall provide notice to Licensor promptly of any such claim, suit, or proceeding and shall assist Licensor, at Licensor's expense, in defending any such claim, suit or proceeding.

9. General Provisions. This Agreement will be governed by and construed in accordance with the laws of the United States and the State of _____ as applied to agreements entered into and to be performed entirely within that state between residents of that state. This Agreement, including any Exhibits to this Agreement, constitutes the entire agreement between the parties relating to this subject matter and supersedes all prior or simultaneous representations, discussions, negotiations, and agreements, whether written or oral. The Agreement may not be modified except by written instrument signed by both parties. No term or provision hereof will be considered waived by either party, and no breach excused by either party, unless such waiver or consent is in writing signed on behalf of the party against whom the waiver is asserted. No consent by either party to, or waiver of, a breach by either party, whether express or implied, will constitute a consent to, waiver of, or excuse of any other, different, or subsequent breach by either party. Licensee may assign its rights and obligations under this Agreement. This Agreement will be for the benefit of Licensee's successors and assigns, and will be binding on Licensor's heirs, legal representatives and permitted assignees. If any dispute arises between the parties with respect to the matters covered by this Agreement which leads to a proceeding to resolve such dispute, the prevailing party in such proceeding shall be entitled to receive its reasonable attorneys' fees, expert witness fees and out-of-pocket costs incurred in connection with such proceeding, in addition to any other relief to which it may be entitled. All notices, requests and other communications required to be given under this Agreement must be in writing, and must be mailed by registered or certified mail, postage prepaid and return receipt requested, or delivered by hand to the party to whom such notice is required or permitted to be given. Any such notice will be considered to have been given when received, or if mailed, five (5) business days after it was mailed, as evidenced by the postmark. The mailing address for notice to either party will be the address shown on the signature page of this Agreement. Either party may change its mailing address by notice as provided by this Section. The following provisions shall survive termination of this Agreement: Sections 7 and 8.

## Content License (Text)

This Agreement is effective as of _____, 19_____.

By: _____    By: _____

_____    _____
Typed name                                                                                                         Typed name

_____    _____
Title                                                                                                                       Title

_____    _____

_____    _____
Address                                                                                                                 Address

# FORM 3

# Content License

## (Photos And Video)

FOUND SOME GREAT PHOTOS or video footage for your Web site, intranet, or online product? If so, you probably need this form. Although some older photos and (rarely) video may be in the "public domain," most photos and video are protected by copyright (even if they don't have copyright notices). Moreover, photos and videos that are in the public domain in the United States may be protected by copyright in other countries. If you use copyrighted photos or video footage without getting a license—permission from the copyright owner—you may find yourself facing a copyright infringement lawsuit.

You also need this form if you shoot or own copyrights in photos or video footage that other people want to use. While your oral grant of permission ("yes, you may use it") would be valid, by using this form you can be specific about what uses of your material you are permitting and for how long.

This form is appropriate for photo licensing and for simple video licensing—for example, for getting permission to use footage owned by an independent video producer, as well as footage from travel videos, corporate training and marketing videos, media libraries, or stock

**Cross-References**

For a discussion of the applicable laws for Form 3, see the following sections in the Overview: Copyright Law, Copyright Licenses, Copyright Ownership, Other Intellectual Property Laws, Privacy and Defamation Law, and Contracts Law.

houses. Licensing footage from motion pictures and television series is much more complex and involves multiple levels of licenses, fees, and performer permissions.

This form assumes that the material is being licensed for nonexclusive use. It also assumes that the material being licensed is already in existence. If a photographer or video producer is being hired to shoot photos or footage, use Form 1 (and the producer should obtain privacy releases such as Form 5, if releases are needed).

This form refers to the copyright owner as "Licensor" and to the party receiving permission to use the licensed photo or video footage as "Licensee." The material being licensed is "the Work." The projects or products in which the licensee is permitted to use "the Work" is "the Project."

Using this form protects you from copyright infringement lawsuits. However, the use of the videos or photographs may lead to liability of other rights: For example, if photos or footage invade the privacy of an individual or make false and negative statements about someone, you may be liable for invasion of privacy, misappropriation of the right of publicity, or defamation.

## Checklist Of Issues

1. What is being licensed (Section 1, "The Work")? To avoid later disputes, be as specific as possible. Here's an example of what should go in the blank in Section 1:

    "the photograph entitled 'A View of San Francisco from Oakland'"

    If it is possible, the parties may wish to attach the photographs or the video footage to the agreement. If the copyright for the photographs or the video has been registered with the Copyright Office, it may be identified by reference to the registration. If excerpts from a video—rather than the whole thing—are being licensed, the agreement should make that clear.

2. In what projects or products will the Licensee be permitted to use the licensed photo or video? This information goes in Section 2 and is called the Project. For example, is Licensee getting the right to use the material on Licensee's Web site or intranet? In an online encyclopedia? In marketing material, including "print media" material?

    Here's an example of what should go in the blank in Section 2:

    "The Web site operated by or for Licensee at the URL www.newsite.com and marketing material in any media relating to such Web site."

3. What rights are being granted (Section 3)? As written, Section 3 provides for a broad grant of rights. If the Project includes a Web site, Section 3 gives Licensee the right to permit end users of the Web site to make one copy of the licensed photo or video for personal, noncommercial use. If the Project includes an internal network (intranet), Section 3 gives Licensee's employees the right to copy the licensed material for Licensee's internal business purpose.

4. Is the license exclusive or nonexclusive? Modify Section 3 if the license is to be exclusive.

5. Will Licensor get a credit? If so, how will it read (Section 4)?

6. What is the license fee (Section 5?) It could be a single one-time fee or an annual fee for each year Licensee uses the Work. The license fee does not have to be money. It could be products or services, publicity, or just a credit.

7. What is the term (duration) of the license (Section 6)? It can be perpetual or limited in duration.

8. What warranties is Licensor giving (Section 7)?

9. What remedy will Licensee have if the Work is not as warranted (Section 8)?

10. Does the photo or video footage prominently show other copyrighted works, such as sculptures or paintings? If so, Licensee will need a license from the owner of the copyright on the separate work, unless the Licensor has already obtained a broad enough license from the owner of that copyright to cover Licensee's use.

11. For video only: Does the video include music owned by a third party? If so, Licensee needs a separate license or licenses to use the music unless Licensee has already obtained a broad enough license to the music to cover Licensee's use. Both musical compositions and sound recordings are protected by copyright.

12. Does the photo or video footage show recognizable individuals? If so, Licensee may need a privacy/publicity release in addition to this copyright license unless the Licensor already obtained one that will cover Licensee's use (see Form 5). Also, Licensee should consider whether using the photo or video footage could be defamatory.

13. Does the photo or video footage show other companies' trademarks? If so, Licensee may need permission from the trademark owners.

14. Does the video include the performances of professional actors or writers who may have rights under union contracts (such as Screen Actor's Guild, American Federation of Television and Radio Artists, and Writer's Guild contracts) to receive additional fees for this new use of the material?

## Negotiating Tips: Licensee

■ ***Time Requirements.*** Licensing is a slow process. You may find that some of the photographs and videos you want to use are not available, and you may encounter unexpected delays. For example, using photos or video footage on a Web site requires a worldwide license, and different parties may own rights to the photos or video in different countries.

■ ***Alternatives.*** Don't plan your project around a particular photograph or video unless you are confident that you can obtain a license to use it. The photograph or video may have already been licensed on an exclusive basis, or it may not be available at a reasonable price.

■ ***Definition of "the Project."*** Pay careful attention to Section 2, the "Project." This license will give you the right to use the licensed photograph or video in specific endeavors, as defined in "the Project." If you use the material in an endeavor that is outside the definition of the Project, the license will not protect you. For example, if the license gives you the right to use the licensed photograph in your Web site and you use it in print publications you sell to customers, your license will not protect you.

Before you fill out Section 2, try to think of every way in which you might want to use the licensed photograph or video, now and in the future. For example, you may wish to post the photograph or video on your company's intranet and distribute the material by email. If so, you should describe the Project broadly as "an internal network operated by or for Licensee and its subsidiaries, including distribution by email or other electronic means to employees of Licensee and its subsidiaries as well as display and performance on such network of Licensee and its subsidiaries."

■ ***Grant of Rights.*** The grant of rights (Section 3) in this form gives you broad rights to use the licensed photograph or video. If the Licensor revises the grant of rights or substitutes his or her version, read the rights grant carefully and make certain it meets your needs. Generally, the use of a photograph on a Web site requires only a license to the reproduction, distribution, and public display rights. The use of video footage requires a license to the reproduction, distribution, and public performance rights. However, you also may need additional rights, such as the right to modify the photograph or video for your use.

If you plan to use the licensed photograph or scenes from the video on products such as toys, t-shirts, and coffee mugs, you need ancillary rights (also known as merchandising rights).

Section 3 provides that if the Project includes a Web site, end users of your Web site may download the licensed photo or video footage for their own use. If Licensor insists on limiting "end user" downloading to downloading for personal, noncommercial use (as Section 3 provides), make sure your Web site terms and conditions contain this limitation.

- **Warranties and Indemnity.** You should try to get warranties and an indemnity from the Licensor to ensure that the Licensor has sufficient rights to grant you the rights stated in Section 3 of the agreement (see Sections 7 and 8). These provisions are designed to give you legal recourse against a Licensor whose photograph or video includes material owned by others, or one who has already licensed the rights on an exclusive basis to someone else. If a Licensor provides you with a photograph or a video that infringes a third party's copyright or the right of privacy or publicity, your use of that material in your Web site, intranet, or online products will make you liable for infringement of the third party's copyright (or those other rights), even if you were not aware of the infringement.

## Negotiating Tips: Licensor

- **Definition of The "Project."** You should ensure that Licensee is specific about how Licensee plans to use your photograph or video. You may not want your material used in Licensee's Project, or you may not want to be associated with Licensee's products or services. If Licensee wants to define "the Project" broadly, remember that a license to use a photograph or a video in multiple projects or in a broadly defined, open-ended project generally should cost more than a license to use them in a single, narrowly defined Project.

  Make sure that the definition of the "Project" is not ambiguous. You and Licensee need to agree on what uses of your photograph or video you are authorizing, and Section 2 needs to clearly state that understanding. If you don't understand the Licensee's terminology, get help (legal or technical). Don't sign a license without understanding what uses you are authorizing the Licensee to make of your photograph or video.

- **Grant of Rights.** The grant of rights in Section 3 may be broader than what you want to grant. If so, you need to modify this provision. For example, you may not wish to grant the right to modify your photograph or video (or you may want the right to approve modifications).

  If Licensee wants a broad exclusive license, consider that you will be giving up the right to license the material to others, and charge a higher fee. Perhaps Licensee will be content with a short-duration exclusive license or with a narrow exclusive license—for example, the exclusive right to use the material for Web-based marketing directed at lawyers.

Section 3 states if the Project includes a Web site, end users of the Web site will have the right to download the licensed material for their own use. You should make certain that such downloading is permitted only for the Web site users' personal, noncommercial use (so that you can obtain additional license revenue for commercial uses).

■ *Warranties and Indemnity.* Licensee probably will insist that the contract include representations and warranties from you (see Section 7). Warranty clauses typically include an indemnity provision (such as Section 8) in which the Licensor promises to defend, indemnify, and hold the Licensee harmless for the breach of any of the warranties (in other words, pay for all costs, including attorneys' fees, arising out of the breach of the warranties). Licensees have good reason for asking for warranties and indemnities: If the licensed photograph or video infringes any third-party copyrights, the Licensee will also violate those rights by using the Work (even though innocent of intent to infringe). If the warranty and indemnity provisions make you nervous, try to negotiate for a dollar limit for your exposure on the indemnity—for example, no more than the license fee. The warranty provision includes a warranty that use of the licensed photograph or video will not violate the rights of publicity or privacy of any individual (Section 7(c)). If your photograph or video shows recognizable individuals and you do not have the necessary privacy/publicity releases, delete the words "publicity" and "privacy" from Section 7(c) and make it clear that Licensee has the responsibility for obtaining any necessary releases.

■ *Credit.* You may want to try to get Licensee to agree to include a credit for you when using your photos or video, as Section 4 provides (so that others who want to use your photos or video will know how to find you). If Licensee agrees to a credit, specify in the contract how your credit should read and where it should be placed. If you have a Web site, you may want the credit to include a link to your Web site.

# PHOTO AND VIDEO FOOTAGE LICENSE AGREEMENT

This agreement is made and entered into by and between _____ ("Licensor") and _____ ("Licensee") on the _____ (the "Effective Date").

NOW, THEREFORE, in consideration of the promises and mutual covenants and agreements set forth herein, the parties agree as follows:

1. DESCRIPTION OF WORK BEING LICENSED: _____
_____ (the "Work").

2. DESCRIPTION OF PROJECTS OR PRODUCTS TO WHICH LICENSE APPLIES: _____ (the "Project").

3. GRANT OF RIGHTS: For good and valuable consideration, the receipt and sufficiency of which are hereby acknowledged, Licensor hereby grants to Licensee a nonexclusive license to reproduce, digitize, edit without destroying the historical integrity or compromising the images, publicly perform, publicly display, and distribute the Work in the Project and in any advertising and promotion related to the Project. If the Project includes an internal network, this license includes the right of employees of Licensee and its subsidiaries to copy the work from the network for Licensee's internal business purposes. If the Project includes a Web site, this license includes the right to permit users of the Web site to reproduce one copy of the Work for their personal, noncommercial use, and Licensee shall so state in its Web site conditions of usage. This license shall not include the right to use the Work independently of the Project or advertising and promotion related thereto. The rights granted herein shall not confer in Licensor any rights of ownership in the Project, including, without limitation, the copyright thereto, all of which shall be and remain the exclusive property of Licensee, except that Licensor shall retain copyright in the Work.

4. CREDIT: In consideration of the rights granted to Licensee, and provided the Work is used in the Project, Licensee agrees to give Licensor credit in writing in the Project in substantially the following form: _____

Any inadvertent failure to provide credit shall not be deemed a breach of this Agreement.

5. LICENSE FEE: In further consideration of the rights granted to Producer herein, Producer shall pay to Licensor the sum of $_____.

6. TERM. This license begins on _____ and ends on _____

7. WARRANTIES. Licensor represents and warrants that:

(a) the Work was created solely by him, his full-time employees during the course of their employment, or independent contractors who assigned all right, title and interest worldwide in their work to the Licensor or Licensor has obtained sufficient rights to grant the license in Section 3;

(b) Licensor is the owner of all right, title and interest in the tangible forms of the Work and all intellectual property rights protecting them or has the right to grant the license in Section 3. The Work and the intellectual property rights protecting the Work are free and clear of all encumbrances, including, without limitation, security interests, licenses, liens, charges or other restrictions which conflict with the license in Section 3;

(c) The use, public display, public performance, reproduction, distribution, or modification of the Work does not and will not violate the rights of any third parties in the Work including, but not limited to, copyrights, trademarks, publicity and privacy;

(d) The Work is not in the public domain;

(e) The grant of the licenses in Section 3 to the Work does not require the payment of any fees to any third parties (including, without limitation, SAG, AFTRA, or Writer's Guild fees)

(f) Licensor has full power and authority to make and enter into this Agreement.

8. INDEMNIFICATION. Licensor agrees to defend, indemnify, and hold harmless Licensee and their officers, directors, sublicensees, employees and agents, from and against any claims, actions or demands, including without limitation reasonable legal and accounting fees, alleging or resulting from the breach of the warranties in Section 7. Licensee shall provide notice to Licensor promptly of any such claim, suit, or proceeding and shall assist Licensor, at Licensor's expense, in defending any such claim, suit or proceeding.

9. General Provisions. This Agreement will be governed by and construed in accordance with the laws of the United States and the State of _____ as applied to agreements entered into and to be performed entirely within that state between residents of that state. This Agreement, including any Exhibits to this Agreement, constitutes the entire agreement between the parties relating to this subject matter and supersedes all prior or simultaneous representations, discussions, negotiations, and agreements, whether written or oral. The Agreement may not be modified except by written instrument signed by both parties. No term or provision hereof will be considered waived by either party, and no breach excused by either party, unless such waiver or consent is in writing signed on behalf of the party against whom the waiver is asserted. No consent by either party to, or waiver of, a breach by either party, whether express or implied, will constitute a consent to, waiver of, or excuse of any other, different, or subsequent breach by either party. Licensee may assign its rights and obligations under this Agreement. This Agreement will be for the benefit of Licensee's successors and assigns, and will be binding on Licensor's heirs, legal representatives and permitted assignees. If any dispute arises between the parties with respect to the matters covered by this Agreement which leads to a proceeding to resolve such dispute, the prevailing party in such proceeding shall be entitled to receive its reasonable attorneys' fees, expert witness fees and out-of-pocket costs incurred in connection with such proceeding, in addition to any other relief to which it may be entitled. All notices, requests and other communications required to be given under this Agreement must be in writing, and must be mailed by registered or certified mail, postage prepaid and return receipt requested, or delivered by hand to the party to whom such notice is required or permitted to be given. Any such notice will be considered to have been given when received, or if mailed, five (5) business days after it was mailed, as evidenced by the postmark. The mailing address for notice to either party will be the address shown on the signature page of this Agreement. Either party may change its mailing address by notice as provided by this Section. The following provisions shall survive termination of this Agreement: Sections 7 and 8.

## Content License (Photos and Video)

This Agreement is effective as of _____, 19_____.

By: _____  By: _____

Typed name                                         Typed name

Title                                              Title

Address                                            Address

# FORM 4

# Web Site Terms and Conditions of Use

ARE YOU PROVIDING INFORMATION on your Web site? If so, you need Form 4 to tell users of your site how they may use that information and to limit your liability for inaccuracies in the information. If you receive communications from site users, you need Form 4 if you plan to use those communications.

Form 4 states the general terms and conditions under which users may use your Web site and information they find on your Web site. If your Web site has a Chat Room, then you need a Chat Room Agreement as well (Form 8) to tell users the rules for using the Chat Room. If you sell products or license software from your Web site, you need a Clickwrap Agreement (Form 10) stating the terms and conditions of your sale or license.

For this form, there are no issues to be negotiated—you're providing the Web site, and users must accept your rules.

**Cross-References**

For a discussion of the applicable laws for Form 4, see the following sections in the Overview: Copyright Law, Copyright Ownership, Copyright Licenses, Other Intellectual Property Laws, Privacy and Defamation Law, and Contracts Law.

Technically, Form 4 is a contract between you, the Web site owner, and users. But how do you get a user to express assent to your terms and conditions? From a legal point of view, the best way to do this is to (1) put the information in this form on a "terms and conditions of use" screen, which a user must pass through before entering the Web site; (2) make the user do something to show assent to the "terms" before entering the Web site—for example, by registering and typing "I agree"; (3) keep records of the user assents; and (4) give users the option of exiting at the "terms" screen if they do not want to accept those rules.

Does that sound like too much trouble? From a legal viewpoint, the next best thing is to require users to click through a "terms" screen to get to your Web site. The "terms" screen states that using the Web site represents the user's assent to the stated terms. The "click through" requirement is being used for Chat Rooms.

You may think that requiring users to click through the "terms" screen to get to your Web site is too much to ask of users, because it slows them down. After all, you don't want to discourage them from using your site. If that's how you feel, take this approach: Make the user aware that your site has Terms and Conditions by placing a notice on your site's home page, and make it easy for them to click to the "terms" screen. Don't just bury the "terms" screen somewhere on your Web site without mentioning it on your home page.

In the Web Site Terms and Conditions of Use form, the Web site owner is referred to as "the Company." The Web site to which the terms and conditions apply is "the Web Site." The Web site user is referred to as "you." All material of any kind posted on the Web Site is the "Material."

In the following checklist, "you" means the Web site owner.

## Checklist Of Issues

1. Section 1 reminds Web Site users that the Material provided on your Web Site is protected by copyright and that unauthorized use may infringe copyright law and other laws. It states the rules for use of the Material. You may need to provide special rules for the use of certain software or content. If so, the special rules may be posted as "Legal Notices."

2. For more complex Web sites, the Terms and Conditions should state that the rules governing certain aspects of Web sites (such as software downloading and Chat Room use) are provided in separate agreements.

3. Section 1 grants users the right to view and download a single copy of the materials at the Web Site for personal, noncommercial use, as long as all copyright and other proprietary notices are retained. Use of the Materials on a network or on another

Web site is prohibited. If you wish to provide broader or narrower use rights, modify this sentence.

4. If the Web Site includes copyrighted material owned by third parties, make sure that any obligations you have to limit Web Site users' use are addressed in Section 1 of your Terms and Conditions (or in special rules stated in Legal Notices). If, for example, your licenses to use third-party material only authorize you to permit user downloading for personal, noncommercial use—which is common in content licenses—Section 1 must include that restriction on user download rights.

5. You may want to add a sentence to Section 1 telling users how to request permission for commercial use or network use of the Material.

6. Sections 2 and 3 are designed to limit your liability for errors in information in material on your Web Site and for damages resulting from the use of the Web Site or its material. They include a disclaimer of all warranties in the Material and a statement that you are not liable to the users for consequential damages and other damages. Section 7 limits your liability to $100 (but you may want to provide a different limit for software).

7. If the Web Site contains material supplied by third parties, you might want to add to Section 2 a statement that you are not responsible for the content of material provided by third parties.

8. Depending on what industry you are in, special notices might be added to Section 2. For example, the owner of a financial services Web site might include a reminder to users to consult with an investment or tax professional before making investment decisions.

9. Many Web sites permit users to communicate with the Web site operator. If your Web Site provides this function and you want to be able to use the user submissions in the future, you will need a license from the user. Section 4 provides a license. It also states that user submissions are not confidential (so that users cannot claim that you need their permission to disclose the submissions).

10. Section 5 disclaims liability for the content of linked sites operated by third parties. If you wish, you may add a statement requiring that a Web site owner who wants to link to your Site must get your permission in advance.

11. If your Web Site includes software that users can download, you should either add software license provisions to this agreement or include Section 6, which states that the software is made available subject to a separate software license (such as Form 10). If your Web Site provides different types of software, you may need a separate

software license for each type, because you may want to grant different use rights for each type of software.

12. If you are concerned about liability for user postings to your Web Site or user use of Web Site Material, you may want to include a user indemnity such as Section 8. In Section 8, the user agrees to "hold you harmless" against any claims against you arising out of the user's use of the Material and software or the user's breach of the terms of this agreement.

13. Section 9 is appropriate if your Web Site provides software or other material which is subject to export control laws.

# WEB SITE TERMS AND CONDITIONS OF USE

This page states the Terms and Conditions under which you may use this Web Site. Please read this page carefully. If you do not accept the Terms and Conditions stated here, do not use the Web Site. Company may revise these Terms and Conditions at any time by updating this posting. You should visit this page periodically to review the Terms and Conditions, because they are binding on you.

### Section 1. Use of Material.

The Company authorizes you to view and download a single copy of the material on this Web site ("Web Site") solely for your personal, noncommercial use. Special rules may apply to the use of certain software and other items provided on the Web Site. Any such special rules are listed as "Legal Notices" on this Web Site and are incorporated into this Agreement by reference.

The contents of this Web Site, such as text, graphics, images and other material ("Material"), are protected by copyright under both United States and foreign laws. Unauthorized use of the Material may violate copyright, trademark, and other laws. You must retain all copyright and other proprietary notices contained in the original Material on any copy you make of the Material. You may not sell or modify the Material or reproduce, display, publicly perform, distribute, or otherwise use the Material in any way for any public or commercial purpose. The use of the Material on any other Web site or in a networked computer environment for any purpose is prohibited.

If you violate any of these Terms, your permission to use the Material automatically terminates and you must immediately destroy any copies you have made of the Material.

### Section 2. Company's Liability.

The Material may contain inaccuracies or typographical errors. Company makes no representations about the accuracy, reliability, completeness, or timeliness of the Material or about the results to be obtained from using the Web Site and the Material. The use the Web Site and the Material is at your own risk. Changes are periodically made to the Web Site and may be made at any time.

COMPANY DOES NOT WARRANT THAT THE WEB SITE WILL OPERATE ERROR-FREE OR THAT THIS WEB SITE AND ITS SERVER ARE FREE OF COMPUTER VIRUSES AND OTHER HARMFUL GOODS. IF YOUR USE OF THE WEB SITE OR THE MATERIAL RESULTS IN THE NEED FOR SERVICING OR REPLACING EQUIPMENT OR DATA, COMPANY IS NOT RESPONSIBLE FOR THOSE COSTS.

THE WEB SITE AND MATERIAL ARE PROVIDED ON AN 'AS IS' BASIS WITHOUT ANY WARRANTIES OF ANY KIND. THE COMPANY AND ITS SUPPLIERS, TO THE FULLEST EXTENT PERMITTED BY LAW, DISCLAIM ALL WARRANTIES, INCLUDING THE WARRANTY OF MERCHANTABILITY, NON-INFRINGEMENT OF THIRD PARTIES RIGHTS, AND THE WARRANTY OF FITNESS FOR PARTICULAR PURPOSE. COMPANY AND ITS SUPPLIERS MAKE NO WARRANTIES ABOUT THE ACCURACY, RELIABILITY, COMPLETENESS, OR TIMELINESS OF THE MATERIAL, SERVICES, SOFTWARE TEXT, GRAPHICS, AND LINKS.

**Section 3. Disclaimer of Consequential Damages.**

IN NO EVENT SHALL COMPANY, ITS SUPPLIERS, OR ANY THIRD PARTIES MENTIONED AT THIS SITE BE LIABLE FOR ANY DAMAGES WHATSOEVER (INCLUDING, WITHOUT LIMITATION, INCIDENTAL AND CONSEQUENTIAL DAMAGES, LOST PROFITS, OR DAMAGES RESULTING FROM LOST DATA OR BUSINESS INTERRUPTION) RESULTING FROM THE USE OR INABILITY TO USE THE WEB SITE AND THE MATERIAL, WHETHER BASED ON WARRANTY, CONTRACT, TORT, OR ANY OTHER LEGAL THEORY, AND WHETHER OR NOT COMPANY IS ADVISED OF THE POSSIBILITY OF SUCH DAMAGES.

**Section 4.  User Submissions.**

Generally, any communication which you post to the Web Site is considered to be non-confidential. If particular Web pages permit the submission of communications which will be treated by Company as confidential, that fact will be stated in "Legal Notices" on those pages. By posting communications to the Web Site, you automatically grant Company a royalty-free, perpetual, irrevocable nonexclusive license to use, reproduce, modify, publish, edit, translate, distribute, perform, and display the communication alone or as part of other works in any form, media, or technology whether now known or hereafter developed, and to sublicense such rights through multiple tiers of sublicensees.

As a User, you are responsible for your own communications and are responsible for the consequences of their posting. You must not do the following things: Post material that is copyrighted, unless you are the copyright owner or have the permission of the copyright owner to post it; post material that reveals trade secrets, unless you own them or have the permission of the owner; post material that infringes on any other intellectual property rights of others or on the privacy or publicity rights of others; post material that is obscene, defamatory, threatening, harassing, abusive, hateful, or embarrassing to another User or any other person or entity; post a sexually-explicit image; post advertisements or solicitations of business; post chain letters or pyramid schemes; or impersonate another person.

The Company does not represent or guarantee the truthfulness, accuracy, or reliability of any of communications posted by other Users or endorse any opinions expressed by Users. You acknowledge that any reliance on material posted by other Users will be at your own risk.

Company does not screen communications in advance and is not responsible for screening or monitoring material posted by Users. If notified by a User of communications which allegedly do not conform to this Agreement, Company may investigate the allegation and determine in good faith and its sole discretion whether to remove or request the removal of the communication. Company has no liability or responsibility to Users for performance or nonperformance of such activities. Company reserves the right to expel Users and prevent their further access to the Web Site for violating this Agreement or the law and the right to remove communications which are abusive, illegal, or disruptive.

**Section 5.  Links to Other Sites.**

The Web Site contains links to third party Web sites. These links are provided solely as a convenience to you and not as an endorsement by Company of the contents on such third-party Web sites. Company is not responsible for the content of linked third-party sites and does not make any representations regarding the content or accuracy of materials on such third party Web sites. If you decide to access linked third-party Web sites, you do so at your own risk.

**Section 6. Software Licenses.**

All software that is made available for downloading from the Web Site ("Software") is protected by copyright and may be protected by other rights. The use of such software is governed by the terms of the software license agreement or designated "Legal Notice" accompanying such software ("License Agreement"). The downloading and use of such software is conditioned on your agreement to be bound by the terms of the License Agreement.

**Section 7. Limitation of Liability.**

Unless otherwise expressly provided in a Software License or Legal Notice, the aggregate liability for Company to you for all claims arising from the use of the Materials (including Software) is limited to $100.

**Section 8. Indemnity.**

You agree to defend, indemnify, and hold harmless the Company, its officers, directors, employees and agents, from and against any claims, actions or demands, including without limitation reasonable legal and accounting fees, alleging or resulting from your use of the Material (including Software) or your breach of the terms of this Agreement. The Company shall provide notice to you promptly of any such claim, suit, or proceeding and shall assist you, at your expense, in defending any such claim, suit or proceeding.

**Section 9. Export Control.**

The United States controls the export of products and information. You agree to comply with such restrictions and not to export or re-export the Materials (including Software) to countries or persons prohibited under the export control laws. By downloading the Materials (including Software), you are agreeing that you are not in a country where such export is prohibited or are a person or entity to which such export is prohibited. You are responsible for compliance with the laws of your local jurisdiction regarding the import, export, or re-export of the Product.

**Section 10. User Information.**

The Company may use the information it obtains relating to you, including your IP address, name, mailing address, email address and use of the Web Site, for its internal business and marketing purposes and may disclosed the information to third parties for such purposes.

**Section 11. General.**

This Web Site is based in _____(city, state). The Company makes no claims the Materials are appropriate or may be downloaded outside of the United States. Access to the Materials (including Software) may not be legal by certain persons or in certain countries. If you access the Web Site from outside of the United States, you do so at your own risk and are responsible for compliance with the laws of your jurisdiction. This Agreement is governed by the internal substantive laws of the State of _____, without respect to its conflict of laws principles. If any provision of this Agreement is found to be invalid by any court having competent jurisdiction, the invalidity of such provision shall not affect the validity of the remaining provisions of this Agreement, which shall remain in full force and effect. No waiver of any term of this Agreement shall be deemed a further or continuing waiver of such term or any other term. Except as expressly provided in a particular "Legal Notice" or Software License or material on particular Web pages, this Agreement constitutes the entire Agreement between you and the Company with respect to the use of Web Site. Any changes to this Agreement must be made in writing, signed by an authorized representative of the Company.

# FORM 5

# Privacy Release

DO YOU WANT TO USE FOR COMMERCIAL PURPOSES photos or video clips that show recognizable individuals? If so, you need this form to avoid invasion of privacy and right of publicity lawsuits from those shown. Generally, you do not need this form if you are using a photograph of an individual to illustrate a point in a factual article or with a biography of that individual. However, if you use the same photograph to sell a product, you do need this release. If you are uncertain about whether your use is commercial, you should obtain the release.

You also need this form if you shoot photos or video footage that others might want to license for use in their Web sites or online products. Using this form will protect you from privacy/publicity lawsuits, and it will make your material more marketable (because the licensees won't have to worry about getting these releases themselves).

Finally, if you have been asked to give permission for the use of your image, you can use this form to do that—imposing restrictions, if you wish, on how your image can be used.

This form is appropriate for use with "regular people" and with photographic models (models are accustomed to signing such forms). It is not appropriate for clearing

**Cross-References**

For a discussion of the applicable laws for Form 5, see the following sections in the Overview: Copyright Law, Copyright Ownership, Privacy and Defamation Law, Contracts Law.

the rights to use motion picture clips. Licensing motion picture clips and getting permission to use the images of performers shown in those clips is complex and involves multiple levels of licenses, fees, and performer permissions.

Using this form protects you from invasion of privacy and right of publicity lawsuits from people shown in a photo or a video clip. If you do not own the copyright in the photo or video clip, you will need a content license, such as Form 3, as well (to avoid the risk of a copyright infringement lawsuit).

This form refers to the person granting permission (the grantor) as "I" (to make this form user-friendly). The recipient of permission is referred to as "Grantee." The photos or video footage are referred to as "the Material."

## Checklist Of Issues

1. This release is a general one, permitting the grantee to use the grantor's image in any way and in any and all media forever and throughout the world (Section 1). If the grantor is not willing to grant such a broad release, the first paragraph will need to be modified.

2. Normally, a person shown in a photograph or video footage does not own the copyright in the photo or footage (the photographer does; or in the case of a work created by an employee within the scope of employment, the employer does). Section 3 makes it clear that the grantor does not own the copyright in the photos or video footage and that the grantee has any permission it needs from the grantor to use and license the photos and footage throughout the world.

3. Minors lack the legal capacity to enter into contracts. In most states, the legal age for entering into contracts is 18. If this form is to be used to get permission to use a minor's image, the minor's parent or legal guardian should sign it (and you should modify Section 5).

## Negotiating Tips: Grantee

■ ***Broad Grant.*** As written, this is a general release which gives you broad rights to use the grantor's image. If the grantor revises the grant language (Section 1), review it carefully and make certain the new language gives you the permission you need to use the grantor's image in all the ways you might want to use it, now and in the future.

■ ***Consideration.*** Section 1 states that the release is being granted "for valuable consideration received." Consideration is what one party to a contract will get from the other party in return for performing the contract obligations. We recommend that you give the grantor consideration for signing the release, but it doesn't have to be money. In some states, for an employee, continued employment may be sufficient consideration.

## Negotiating Tips: Grantor

- ■ *Association with the Grantee.* If you do not want to be associated with the grantee or the grantee's products or services, don't sign this release.
- ■ *Limiting the Grant.* As currently written, this release permits the grantee to use your image in any way in all media and in any projects or products, forever and throughout the world (Section 1). You might want to limit the grant of permission—restricting the use of your image to use in connection with a particular project or products, for example, or to use for a limited period of time. Or you might want to prohibit its use in connection with other projects or products or prohibit modification of your image.
- ■ *Assignment.* As currently written, this release is assignable by the grantee (meaning that the grantee could authorize a successor company or even an unrelated company to use your photos). If you want tighter control over the use of your image, delete this provision.

## PRIVACY RELEASE

1. GRANT OF RIGHTS. For valuable consideration received, I hereby grant to _____ ("Grantee") the absolute and irrevocable right and permission, throughout the world, in respect of the photographs or video footage ("the Material") that it has, has taken, or has had taken of me or in which I may be included with others:

    (a) To use, re-use, publish, and re-publish, and otherwise reproduce, digitize, edit, modify, distribute, publicly display, and publicly perform the same, in whole or in part, individually or in conjunction with other photographs or videos, and in conjunction with any copyrighted matter, in any and all media now or hereafter known, for illustration, promotion, art, advertising and trade, or any other purpose whatsoever; and

    (b) To use my name in connection with the Material if it so chooses.

2. RELEASE. I hereby release and discharge Grantee from any and all claims and demands arising out of or in connection with the use of the photographs or footage, including without limitation any and all claims for defamation, invasion of privacy, and misappropriation of my right of publicity.

3. COPYRIGHT IN THE MATERIAL. I acknowledge that I have no claim to the copyrights in the Material. The copyright owners have the right to copyright the Material in their own names or otherwise and to use, assign, and license the Material throughout the world, including any rights I might have.

4. ASSIGNMENT OF RELEASE. Grantee may sell, assign, license or otherwise transfer all rights granted to it hereunder. This authorization and release shall also inure to the benefit of the heirs, legal representatives, licensees, and assigns of Grantee, as well as the person(s) (if any) for whom it took the photographs.

5. GRANTOR'S REPRESENTATIONS. I am of full age and have the right to contract in my own name. I have read the foregoing and fully understand the contents thereof. This release shall be binding upon me and my heirs, legal representatives and assigns. I further release Grantee from any responsibility for injury incurred during the photography session.

Signed: _____

Address _____

City, State, Zip _____

Phone _____

Soc.Sec # _____

# FORM 6

# Web Site Development Agreement

Are you hiring a freelance Web developer to create a Web site for you? Or do you develop Web sites for others? If so, you need Form 6.

This form covers Web site development and maintenance. It assumes that Internet access (sometimes called Web hosting) will be provided by a separate Internet service provider who is not a party to this agreement.

The form refers to the party hiring the developer as "the Client" and the party creating the Web site as "the Developer." The form envisions a multistage development process. First, the Developer creates the Web site design. Next, the Developer creates the Beta (working) version of the Web site, tests it, and delivers it to the Client for testing. Finally, the Developer creates the final version and delivers it to the Client for testing.

Although many Web sites involve only text and graphics, more complex Web sites may include software

**Cross-References**

For a discussion of the applicable laws for Form 6, see the following sections in the Overview: Copyright Law, Copyright Ownership, Copyright Licenses, Other Intellectual Property Laws, Privacy and Defamation Law, and Contracts Law.

or "scripts." This form includes references to software which may not be necessary for your project.

The design and technical specifications for the Web site are to be attached as Schedule A. The due dates for the "Deliverables"—the Web site design, Beta Version, and Final Version with Source Material (source code and documentation)—are to be stated in Schedule B. The agreement provides for a "milestone" payment to be made when the contract is signed and when each Deliverable is accepted by the Client.

## Checklist Of Issues

1. What are the technical and design specifications for the contract? They should be as specific as possible. Vagueness can camouflage misunderstanding that will come to light when Developer delivers the material to Client for testing. Detailed specifications serve two purposes: First, the process of creating them helps avoid misunderstandings about the responsibilities of Developer and Client. Second, if there is a dispute later about whether Developer has performed its contractual obligations, the specifications will establish the scope of those obligations.

2. What are the Deliverables (Schedule B)? The typical ones are stated in Schedule B—the Web site design, which is described in Section 2.1; Beta Version; and Final Version with Source Material. These terms are defined in Section 1. Other deliverables can be added—for example, an alpha version (first version).

3. When are the Web site design and other Deliverables due? This information goes on Schedule B.

4. When is payment due? Frequently, payments are made when the contract is signed and upon acceptance of a Deliverable by Client. Will Developer receive a bonus for completion of the Web site by a certain date? This information goes in Schedule B.

5. How is acceptance of Deliverables determined (Section 3.1)? Client testing will occur during an acceptance period: the length of time Client has to test the Deliverable and notify Developer of any errors. Once Client has accepted the Deliverable (or the acceptance period has passed without a rejection notice from Client), the agreement provides that a milestone payment is due (as stated in Schedule B).

6. How long will Developer have to make corrections, if Client requests corrections after testing a Deliverable (Section 3.2)? How long will Client have to test the corrected version? This agreement states that if Client determines, after three attempts at correction by Developer, that the Deliverable is still not acceptable, Client may terminate the agreement.

7. What promises will Developer make about the performance of the Web site? This form contains a Developer warranty (Section 4.1) that the Web site will be of high quality, will be free of defects in material and workmanship in all material respects, and will conform in all respects to the functional and other descriptions contained in the Specifications. Other possible warranties on the Web site's operation could include a warranty that the Web site will operate with named Web browsers or a warranty that it will operate error-free for a stated period of time.

8. What support services will Developer provide during the Warranty Period (defined in Section 4.1 as one year after the date of Client's acceptance of the Final Version)? Is there a limit on how many hours of service Developer must provide per month? This information goes in Section 4.2 and on Schedule D.

9. Is Developer willing to commit to providing maintenance services after the warranty period ends, during a Maintenance Period? How many years will Developer agree to provide these services and for what annual fee? This information goes in Section 4.2. Will Developer also agree to provide new development services to "upgrade" the Web site to use new technologies or change its organization?

10. Who will own the copyright in the Web site as a whole; in individual content components created by Developer for the Web site (graphics and text, for example); and in software created by Developer for use in the Web site? Technically, if the contract says nothing about copyright ownership, Developer automatically owns all the copyrights (and Client has only an implied license of uncertain scope to use the material created by Developer). Although many people believe that ordering and paying for material automatically means that they will own the copyright, they are wrong. The contract should address these ownership issues to avoid misunderstandings. This form states (Section 5.1) that Client will own the Web site content, which is defined in Section 1.13 as the graphic user interface, text, images, music, and other material visible to a Web browser and the software developed by Developer to implement the Web site. If Developer is to retain ownership, Sections 5.1 and 5.2 must be modified to reflect that change and to define what rights Client will have to use the material. Section 5.3 can be used if Developer is to retain ownership of individual content components or software, which could include material created by Developer prior to this project and material created during this project which Developer wants to use in other design projects.

11. What content will be provided by Client? This material—called "Client Content"— should be listed in Schedule C to avoid disputes and misunderstandings about who

provided it and who owns it. In Section 5.5, Client grants Developer a nonexclusive license to reproduce and modify Client Content and Web Site content to develop and maintain the Web site. If Client Content includes any material not owned by Client, licenses with the third-party owners will probably be needed (see Forms 2 and 3). Section 5.7 states that Client must obtain those licenses and pay for them.

12. Who will obtain licenses to use content (other than that listed as Client Content) owned by third-parties, and who will be responsible for licensing costs (Section 5.7)? What about licenses to use Developer Tools (Section 5.8)? What about licenses to use other specified software, such as software for electronic commerce transactions (Section 5.9)?

13. What warranties will Developer and Client provide (Section 8)? If Developer uses content or software owned by others without permission, Client will be liable for infringement for using the material on its Web site. Developer should be responsible for any damages suffered by Client for using the material. If Client provides material (Client Content) the use of which infringes the rights of others, Developer will be liable for using *that* material. Client should be responsible in that case for Developer's damages.

14. What form will Developer's "credit" take? Credits usually consist of Developer's logo and a few lines of text, with a link to Developer's own Web site. Three possibilities are: a "footer" credit, in which the credit runs at the bottom of each Web page; a "banner" credit, in which the credit is displayed on a banner on one or more pages of the site; and an "acknowledgments page" credit, in which the credit appears only on a single page. This information goes in Schedule E.

## Negotiating Tips: Client

- ***Specifications (Schedule A).*** Developer needs to understand what features you want in your Web site in order to create the Specifications. If you don't know what you want, you should spend some time on the Internet reviewing existing sites. Look at other sites designed by Developer. Talk to Web site owners about what has worked for them. Read up on Web marketing (or hire a Web marketing consultant). If you don't understand the terminology used in the Specifications, get help. Don't sign the contract without understanding what you need and what Developer is promising.

- ***Copyright Ownership.*** Generally, you should try to obtain ownership of copyrights in all material created for you by Developer. If you do so, you will then have all the copyright owner's exclusive rights in the material—including the right to use the material in later projects and different media and the right to modify the material. However, you should understand that in certain situations Developer may resist giving you outright ownership. If Developer is to retain copyright ownership of all or part of the Web site, you should make certain that the contract gives you the right to use and modify the material owned by Developer in every way and every media that you believe will be necessary, both now and in the future.

If you and Developer cannot agree on the allocation of copyright ownership, you may be able to compromise by letting Developer retain copyright ownership of particular content components or software while giving you copyright ownership of the rest of the Web site (see Section 5.3).

■ ***Developer's Warranties and Indemnities.*** You should try to get warranties and an indemnity from Developer (see Section 8). The warranties ensure that (1) Developer has created the Web site alone, so that Developer can assign you ownership of the copyright in the Web site or license you the rights to the Web site; (2) Developer has not used preexisting materials owned by third parties. If Developer uses material in your Web site that infringes a third party's copyrights or other rights, your use of the material in your Web site will make you liable for infringement, even if you were not aware of the infringement.

■ ***Your Warranties.*** Before you warrant that Client Content is not infringing or defamatory (Section 8.5(c)), review the Client Content material carefully (and read Copyright Law, Copyright Ownership, Copyright Licenses, and Privacy and Defamation Law in the Overview). While you own the copyright in material that was created for you by your full-time employees within the scope of their employment, you do not own the copyright in the material that was created for you by an independent contractor unless you obtained an assignment or a valid work for hire agreement.

Don't assume that your company owns the copyright in a work because the company has used it before. The past use may have been unauthorized. And don't assume that you have the right to use material in your Web site because you licensed it in the past for other uses. The old license may not cover use of the material in your Web site.

■ ***Domain Name.*** If you haven't already registered the domain name you will be using for your Web site, you should either register it yourself or have your Internet Service Provider register it for you. If Developer will be registering your domain name for you, you should make certain that you are listed as the registrant. Otherwise, Developer will be able to transfer the domain name to another individual or company.

■ *Services of an Individual.* If you enter into a contract with a Developer which is a corporation and expect to obtain the services of particular individuals employed by the corporation, the contract should state that the work can be done only by the named individuals. Otherwise, the corporation will be free to use any of its employees to do the job.

## Negotiating Tips: Developer

■ *Deadlines.* You should make certain that the deadlines for the Deliverables (stated in Schedule B) are realistic. If you deliver the Deliverables late, Client may terminate the contract and not pay you. Normally, Client will have no obligation to reimburse you for any of your costs if Client is entitled to terminate the contract.

■ *Specifications.* If you are dealing with a client who is a Web novice, you should educate the client about Web sites and show the client samples of your work before the client signs this contract. Make certain Client understands what you are promising to do in the Specifications.

■ *Acceptance Clause.* For your protection, the proposal and contract should provide a procedure and a deadline for Client objections to the delivered Work Product (see Section 3.1). You need to know that after a certain period of time passes, it will be too late for the Client to say, "I won't accept this. Do it again."

■ *Third-Party Content Licenses.* If Client is expecting you to use expensive content—an excerpt of Madonna singing "Like a Virgin," for example, or a photo of a famous person—the contract should state who is responsible for obtaining permission to use such rights. If it will be your responsibility to obtain these licenses, you should raise your price to cover the costs of obtaining such rights. Those costs include personnel time to negotiate the rights and the license fees. Be careful not to commit yourself to obtaining rights to use specific content, because those works may not be available.

■ *Copyright Ownership.* If you agree to assign the copyright in the material you create to Client, you will not be able to use any of that material in other projects or modify it for other projects. Once you assign the copyright, Client will have the copyright owner's exclusive rights to reproduce the work, distribute it, publicly perform it, publicly display it, and modify it for use in derivative works. However, you will still be able to re-use ideas that you used in the material.

If you are creating material to fill Client's special needs, you may not object to giving Client ownership of the copyright (particularly if Client is willing to pay a higher fee for an assignment of all rights). You may, however, want to retain copyright ownership of some components—for example, certain graphics, or a "shopping cart" program for online sales transactions. You can use Section 5.3 to do that. Unless you retain copyright ownership of the components or get a license from Client to re-use them, your use of the components in future projects will infringe Client's copyright.

If the copyright is owned by Client, you may want to include a clause in the contract authorizing you to make demonstration copies of the Web site to show to future clients. Or you may want a license back to make limited use of certain components in other projects.

■ ***Warranties and Indemnity.*** Client will probably insist that the contract include representations and warranties from you (see Section 8.1). Warranty clauses typically include an indemnity provision in which Developer promises to defend, indemnify, and hold Client harmless for the breach of any of the warranties (in other words, pay for all costs, including attorneys' fees, arising out of the breach of the warranties). Clients have good reason for asking for warranties and indemnities: If you infringe any third-party intellectual property rights in creating Client's Web site, Client will become an infringer by posting the Web site (even though innocent of intent to infringe). If the warranty and indemnity provisions make you nervous, try to negotiate a dollar limit for your exposure on the indemnity—for example, no more than your total compensation for the development of the Web site.

■ ***Termination Clause.*** This contract, as written, can be terminated by Client at any time (Section 9.2). If Client terminates, Client has to pay you for work done up to that point. You may want to try to negotiate for a termination fee—or limit Client's right to terminate.

# WEB SITE DEVELOPMENT AND MAINTENANCE AGREEMENT

This Agreement is entered into by and between _____ ("Client") and _____ ("Developer") on the _____(the "Effective Date").

RECITALS

WHEREAS, Developer has experience in developing and maintaining Web sites for third parties;

WHEREAS, Client wishes to have Developer create a Web site for Client and maintain such Web site for Client, and Developer is interested in undertaking such work.

WHEREAS, Client shall employ a separate company to host its Web site.

NOW, THEREFORE, in consideration of the promises and mutual covenants and agreements set forth herein, Client and Developer agree as follows:

## Section 1
## DEFINITIONS

1.1 **Beta Version** means a working version of the Web Site recorded in executable form on the specified medium with any necessary supporting software and data, which has been fully tested by Developer prior to delivery and which Developer believes in good faith to be bug free and to fully implement all functions called for in the Specifications.

1.2 **Client Content** means the material provided by Client to be incorporated into the Web Site, as listed on Schedule "C."

1.3 **Development Schedule** shall be as set forth in Schedule "B" to this Agreement which lists the deliverable items contracted for ("Deliverables") and the deadlines for their delivery. "Payment Schedule" shall be as also set forth in Schedule "B".

1.4 **Developer Tools** means the software tools of general application, whether owned or licensed to Developer, which are used to develop the Web Site.

1.5 **Documentation** means the documentation for the software developed by Developer specifically for the Web Site and other material which implement the Web Site. Source materials are part of the Documentation.

1.6 **Enhancements** means any improvements to the Web Site to implement new features or add new material. Enhancements shall include modifications to the Web Site Content to make the Web Site operate on a Server System of a new ISP.

1.7 **Error** means any failure of the Web Site (i) to meet the Specifications and/or (ii) to operate with the Server System.

1.8 **Final Version** means a non-copy protected and unencrypted disk master of the final version of the Web Site, recorded in executable form on the specified medium with any necessary supporting software and data, as to which all development work hereunder, and corrections to the Beta Version, have been completed and which meets the Specifications.

1.9 **ISP** means an Internet Service Provider which maintains the Web Site on the World Wide Web portion of the Internet. The ISP may change from time to time.

1.10 **Specifications** for the Web Site shall be as set forth in Schedule "A" to this Agreement.

1.11 **Source Materials** means (i) all documentation, notes, development aids, technical documentation and other materials provided to Developer by Client for use in developing the Web Site, and (ii) the source code, documentation, notes and other materials which are produced or created by Developer during the development of the Web Site, in such internally documented form as is actually used by Developer for development and maintenance of the Web Site.

1.12 **Server System** means the hardware and software system owned or licensed by the ISP.

1.13 **Web Site Content** shall mean (i) the graphic user interface, text, images, music and other material of the Web Site developed by Developer under this Agreement which is visible to World Wide Web browsers and (ii) software (including cgi scripts and perl scripts) developed by Developer under this Agreement to implement the Web Site. Web Site Content shall not include Developer Tools.

1.14 **Web Site** means the site to be developed for Client on the graphic portion of the Internet known as the World Wide Web which is described in the Specifications.

## Section 2
## DEVELOPMENT AND DELIVERY OF DELIVERABLES

2.1 **Development; Progress Reports.** Developer shall use its best efforts to develop each Deliverable in accordance with the Specifications. Developer shall first prepare a design for the Web Site. This design shall include drawings of the user interface, a schematic of how to navigate the Web Site, a list of hyperlinks and other components. All development work will be performed by Developer or its employees at Developer's offices or by approved independent contractors who have executed confidentiality and assignment agreements which are acceptable to Client. Developer agrees that no development work shall be performed by independent contractors without the express written approval of Client. Each week following execution of this Agreement during which any development and/or testing hereunder remains uncompleted, and whenever else Client shall reasonably request, Developer shall contact, or meet with Client's representative, and report all tasks completed and problems encountered relating to development and testing of the Web Site. During such discussion or meeting, Developer shall advise Client in detail of any recommended changes with respect to remaining phases of development in view of Developer's experience with the completed development. In addition, Developer shall contact Client's representative promptly by telephone upon discovery of any event or problem that will materially delay development work, and thereafter, if requested, promptly confirm such report in writing.

2.2 **Delivery.** Developer shall deliver all Deliverables for the Web Site within the times specified in the Development Schedule and in accordance with the Specifications.

2.3 **Manner of Delivery.** Developer agrees to comply with all reasonable requests of Client as to the manner of delivery of all Deliverables, which may include delivery by electronic means.

2.4 **Delivery of Source Materials.** Upon request by Client, but in no event later than the delivery of the Final Version, Developer shall deliver to Client all Source Materials.

## Section 3
## TESTING AND ACCEPTANCE; EFFECT OF REJECTION

3.1 **Testing and Acceptance Procedure.** All Deliverables shall be thoroughly tested by Developer and all necessary corrections as a result of such testing shall be made, prior to delivery to Client. Upon receipt of a Deliverable, Client shall have a period of ____ days within which to test the item ("the Acceptance Period") and to notify Developer in writing of its acceptance or rejection based on its test results with respect thereto. If Client has not given notice of rejection within the Acceptance Period, the Deliverable will be deemed to be accepted. No delivery of a Deliverable shall be considered complete unless and until Client has received all Documentation necessary to support the use and modification of the Deliverable. If Client accepts the Deliverable, the milestone payment for that Deliverable (set forth in Schedule "B") is then due.

3.2 **Correction.** If Client requests that Developer correct errors in the Deliverable, Developer shall within ____ days of such notice, or such longer period as Client may allow, submit at no additional charge a revised Deliverable in which such Errors have been corrected. Upon receipt of the corrected Deliverable, Client shall have an additional days to test the Deliverable and either (1) accept it (making the milestone payment set out in Schedule "B"); or (2) request that Developer make further corrections to the Deliverable to meet the Specifications and repeat the correction and review procedure set forth in this Paragraph 3.2. In the event Client determines, in its sole discretion, that the Deliverable continues to include Errors after three attempts at correction by Developer, Client may terminate this Agreement.

## Section 4
## OTHER OBLIGATIONS OF DEVELOPER

4.1 **Web Site Warranty.** Developer represents and warrants that the Web Site (1) will be of high quality and free of defects in material and workmanship in all material respects; and (2) will conform in all respects to the functional and other descriptions contained in the Specifications. For a period of one year after the date of acceptance of the Final Version by Client ("the Warranty Period"), Developer agrees to fix at its own expense any Errors. EXCEPT AS STATED IN SECTION 8.1, DEVELOPER DISCLAIMS ALL IMPLIED WARRANTIES, INCLUDING WITHOUT LIMITATION, THE WARRANTIES OF MERCHANTABILITY, NON-INFRINGEMENT OF THIRD PARTY RIGHTS, AND FITNESS FOR A PARTICULAR PURPOSE.

4.2 **Web Site Support.** Developer also agrees to provide Client with the support services stated in Schedule D to maintain and update the Web Site on the World Wide Web during the Warranty Period at no cost to Client. Such assistance shall not exceed __ hours per calendar month.

4.3 **Maintenance Period.** After the expiration of the Warranty Period, Developer agrees to provide Client with the services stated in Schedule D, at Client's option, for _____ years after the last day of the Warranty Period ("the Maintenance Period") for an annual fee of _____. Such maintenance shall include correcting any Errors or any failure of the Web Site to conform to the Specifications. Maintenance shall not include the development of Enhancements at the time of the notice.

4.4 **Enhancements.** During the Maintenance Period, if Developer wishes to modify the Web Site, it may request that Developer provide a bid to provide such Enhancements. Developer shall provide Client a first priority on its resources to create the Enhancements over any other third party with the exception of obligations under contracts with third parties existing on the date of the notice. Such services shall be provided on a time and materials basis at the most favored price under which Developer provides such services to third parties.

## Section 5
## PROPRIETARY RIGHTS

5.1 **Client's Ownership Rights.** Developer acknowledges and agrees that except as stated in Section 5.3, the Web Site Content and Documentation, including but not limited to images, graphic user interface, source and object code, and any documentation and notes associated with the Web Site are and shall be the property of Client. Title to all intellectual property rights including but not limited to copyrights, trademarks, patents and trade secrets in the Web Site Content and Documentation is with, and shall remain with Client.

5.2 **Assignment of Rights.** Except as provided in Section 5.3, Developer hereby irrevocably assigns, conveys and otherwise transfers to Client, and its respective successors and assigns, all rights, title and interests worldwide in and to the Web Site Content and Documentation and all copyrights, trade secrets, patents, trademarks and other intellectual property rights and all contract and licensing rights, and all claims and causes of action of any kind with respect to any of the foregoing, whether now known or hereafter to become known. In the event Developer has any rights in and to the Web Site Content or Documentation that cannot be assigned to Client, Developer hereby unconditionally and irrevocably waives the enforcement of all such rights, and all claims and causes of action of any kind with respect to any of the foregoing against Client, its distributors and customers, whether now known or hereafter to become known and agrees, at the request and expense of Client and its respective successors and assigns, to consent to and join in any action to enforce such rights and to procure a waiver of such rights from the holders of such rights. In the event Developer has any rights in and to the Web Site Content or Documentation that cannot be assigned to Client and cannot be waived, Developer hereby grants to Client, and its respective successors and assigns, an exclusive, worldwide, royalty-free license during the term of the rights to reproduce, distribute, modify, publicly perform and publicly display, with the right to sublicense through multiple tiers of sublicensees and assign such rights in and to the Web Site Content and the Documentation including, without limitation, the right to use in any way whatsoever the Web Site Content and Documentation. Developer retains no rights to use the Web Site Content and Documentation except as stated in Section 5.3 and agrees not to challenge the validity of the copyright ownership by Client in the Web Site Content and Documentation.

5.3. **Ownership of Components.** Contractor will retain copyright ownership of the following material: _____ ("Retained Components"). However, Contractor grants to Client a royalty-free, worldwide, perpetual, irrevocable, nonexclusive license, with the right to sublicense through multiple tiers of sublicensees, to use, reproduce, distribute, modify, publicly perform, and publicly display the Retained Components on the Web Site or any Web site operated by or for Client and related marketing material.

5.4 **Power of Attorney.** Developer agrees to execute, when requested, patent, copyright, or similar applications and assignments to Client, and any other lawful documents deemed necessary by Client to carry out the purpose of this Agreement. Developer further agrees that the obligations and undertaking stated in this Section 5.4 will continue beyond the termination of this Agreement. In the event that Client is unable for any reason whatsoever to secure Developer's signature to any lawful and necessary document required to apply for or execute any patent, copyright or other applications with respect to the Web Site Content and Documentation (including improvements, renewals, extensions, continuations, divisions or continuations in part thereof), Developer hereby irrevocably designates and appoints Client and its duly authorized officers and agents as his agents and attorneys-in-fact to act for and in his behalf and instead of Developer, to execute and file any such application and to do all other lawfully permitted acts to further the prosecution and issuance of patents, copyrights or other rights thereon with the same legal force and effect as if executed by Developer.

5.5 **License to Web Site Content and Client Content.** Client grants to Developer a nonexclusive, worldwide license to reproduce and modify Client Content and the Web Site Content to develop and maintain the Web Site.

5.6 **Internet Access.** Client shall be responsible for obtaining access to the Internet through an ISP. Developer shall not be responsible for such access and shall not be considered a party to the agreement between ISP and Client. Although the Web Site will be hosted by the ISP, the ISP will not be a party to this Agreement nor will it be a third party beneficiary of this Agreement.

5.7 **Licenses to Third-Party Content.** _____ shall be responsible for obtaining and paying for any necessary licenses to use third-party content other than the third-party content listed on Schedule C as Client Content. Client shall be responsible for obtaining and paying for any necessary licenses to use third-party content listed on Schedule C.

5.8. **Licenses to Developer Tools.** Developer shall be responsible for obtaining licenses for and paying license fees for any Developer Tools used in this project that are not owned by Developer.

5.9. **Licenses to Use Other Software.** _____ shall be responsible for obtaining a license to use _____ software and for paying license fees for such software.

5.10 **Client's Domain Name.** Client's domain name, _____, shall remain the sole property of Client. Developer acknowledges that Developer has no right to use Client's domain name other than in connection with the Web Site development and maintenance project covered in this Agreement.

## Section 6
## PAYMENT

6.1 **Payment Schedule.** The fees set forth in Schedule "B" shall be paid as provided in such Schedule.

6.2 **Maintenance Fees.** If Client chooses to have Developer perform maintenance and support service during the Maintenance Period, the annual fee stated in Section 4.3 shall be due thirty (30) days prior to the commencement date of each year of the Maintenance Period.

6.3 **Taxes.** Developer shall be responsible for the payment of all sales, use and similar taxes.

6.4 **Expenses.** Except as expressly stated in this Agreement or in a later writing signed by Client, Developer shall bear all expenses arising from the performance of its obligations under this Agreement.

## Section 7
## CONFIDENTIALITY

7.1 **Confidential Information.** The terms of this Agreement, the Source Materials and technical and marketing plans or other sensitive business information, including all materials containing said information, which are supplied by Client to Developer or developed by Developer in the course of developing the Web Site is the confidential information ("Confidential Information") of Client.

7.2 **Restrictions on Use.** Developer agrees that except as authorized in writing by Client: (i) Developer will preserve and protect the confidentiality of all Confidential Information; (ii) Developer will not disclose to any third party, the existence, source, content or substance of the Confidential Information or make copies of Confidential Information; (iii) Developer will not deliver Confidential Information to any third party, or permit the Confidential Information to be removed from Developer's premises; (iv) Developer will not use Confidential Information in any way other than to develop the Web Site as provided in this Agreement; (v) Developer will not disclose, use or copy any third party information or materials received in confidence by Developer for purposes of work performed under this Agreement; and (vi) Developer shall require that each of its employees who work on or have access to the Confidential Information to sign a suitable confidentiality and assignment agreement and be advised of the confidentiality and other applicable provisions of this Agreement.

7.3 **Limitations.** Information shall not be considered to be Confidential Information if Developer can demonstrate that it (i) is already or otherwise becomes publicly known through no act of Developer; (ii) is lawfully received from third parties subject to no restriction of confidentiality; (iii) can be shown by Developer to have been independently developed by it without use of the Confidential Information; or (iv) is authorized in writing by Client to be disclosed, copied or used.

7.4 **Return of Source Materials.** Upon Client's acceptance of the Final Version, or upon Client's earlier request, Developer shall provide Client with all copies and originals of the Web Site Content, Client Content and Source Materials, as well as any other materials provided to Developer, or created by Developer under this Agreement. Not later than seven (7) days after the termination of this Agreement for any reason, or if sooner requested by Client, Developer will return to Client all originals and copies of the Confidential Information, Web Site Content, Client Content and Source Materials, as well as any other materials provided to Developer, or created by Developer under this Agreement, except that Developer may retain one copy of the Web Site Content and Source Materials, which will remain the Confidential Information of Client, for the sole purpose of assisting Developer in maintaining the Web Site. Developer shall return said copy to Client promptly upon request by Client.

## Section 8
## WARRANTIES COVENANTS AND INDEMNIFICATION

8.1 **Warranties and Covenants of Developer.** Developer represents, warrants and covenants to Client the following:

(a) Developer has the full power to enter into this Agreement and perform the services provided for herein, and that such ability is not limited or restricted by any agreements or understandings between Developer and other persons or companies;

(b) Any information or materials developed for, or any advice provided to Client, shall not rely or in any way be based upon confidential or proprietary information or trade secrets obtained or derived by Developer from sources other than Client unless Developer has received specific authorization in writing to use such proprietary information or trade secrets;

(c) Except to the extent based on Client Content used as licensed to Developer in Section 5.5 and on licenses obtained by Client pursuant to Sections 5.7 and 5.9, the use, public display, public performance, reproduction, distribution, or modification of the Web Site Content and Documentation does not and will not violate the rights of any third parties, including, but not limited to, copyrights, trade secrets, trademarks, publicity, privacy, and patents. The use of the Developer Tools in the Web Site Content and Documentation does not and will not violate the rights of any third parties, including but not limited to, copyrights, trade secrets, trademarks, publicity, privacy, and patents;

(d) Its performance of this Agreement will not conflict with any other contract to which Developer is bound, and while developing the Web Site, Developer will not engage in any such consulting services or enter into any agreement in conflict with this Agreement.

(e) The Web Site Content and the Documentation was created solely by Developer, Developer's full-time employees during the course of their employment, or independent contractors who assigned all right, title and interest worldwide in their work to Contractor.

(f) Developer is the owner of all right, title and interest in the tangible forms of the Web Site Content and Documentation and all intellectual property rights protecting them. The Web Site Content and Documentation and the intellectual property rights protecting them are free and clear of all encumbrances, including, without limitation, security interests, licenses, liens, charges or other restrictions.

(g) Contractor has maintained the Source Material in confidence.

(h) The Web Site Content and the Documentation is not in the public domain.

8.3 **Developer's Indemnity.** Developer agrees to defend indemnify and hold harmless Client and its directors, officers, its employees, sublicensees, and agents from and against all claims, defense costs (including reasonable attorneys' fees), judgments and other expenses arising out of or on account of such claims, including without limitation claims of:

(a) alleged infringement or violation of any trademark, copyright, trade secret, right of publicity or privacy (including but not limited to defamation), patent or other proprietary right with respect to the Web Site Content or Documentation unless based on the use of the Client Content or on licenses obtained by Client pursuant to sections 5.7 and 5.9;

(b) any use of confidential or proprietary information or trade secrets Developer has obtained from sources other than Client;

(c) any negligent act, omission, or willful misconduct of Developer in the performance of this Agreement; and

(d) the breach of any covenant or warranty set forth in Section 8.1 above.

8.4 **Obligations Relating to Indemnity.** Developer's obligation to indemnify requires that Client notify Developer promptly of any claim as to which indemnification will be sought and provide Developer reasonable cooperation in the defense and settlement thereof.

8.5 **Client's Indemnification.** Client agrees to defend, indemnify, and hold harmless Developer and its directors, officers, its employees and agents from and against all claims, defense costs (including reasonable attorneys' fees), judgments and other expenses arising out of the breach of the following covenants and warranties:

(a) Client possesses full power and authority to enter into this Agreement and to fulfill its obligations hereunder.

(b) The performance of the terms of this Agreement and of Client's obligations hereunder shall not breach any separate agreement by which Client is bound.

(c) The use, public display, public performance, reproduction, distribution, or modification of Client Content in accordance with the license granted to Developer in Section 5.5 does not and will not violate the rights of any third parties including, but not limited to, copyrights, trade secrets, trademarks, publicity, privacy, and patents. The use of third-party licensed material obtained by Client pursuant to Sections 5.7 and 5.9, if within the scope of the license, does not violate the rights of any third parties, including, but not limited to, copyrights, trade secrets, trademarks, publicity, privacy, defamation, and patents.

8.6 **Obligations Relating to Indemnity.** Client's obligation to indemnify requires that Developer notify Client promptly of any claim as to which indemnification will be sought and provide Client reasonable cooperation in the defense and settlement thereof.

## Section 9
## TERMINATION

9.1 **Termination for Non-Performance or Delay.** In the event of a termination of this Agreement by Client pursuant to Paragraph 3.2 hereof, Client will have no further obligations or liabilities under this Agreement. Client will have the right, in addition to all of its other rights, to require Developer to deliver to Client all of Developer's work in progress, including all originals and copies thereof, as well as any other materials provided to Developer by Client or third parties, or created by Developer under this Agreement. Developer may keep any milestone payments which have been paid or are due under Schedule "B", and such payments shall be deemed payment in full for all obligations of Client under this Agreement, including full payment for all source code, object code, documentation, notes, graphics and all other materials and work relating to the portion of the Web Site and the assignment or licenses of rights relating to the Web Site which has been completed as of the time of termination.

9.2 **Termination for Convenience.** Client shall have the right at any time to terminate this Agreement upon fifteen (15) days notice by giving written notice of termination to Developer. Developer shall immediately cease all work on the Web Site. In the event of such termination, Client's entire financial obligation to Developer shall be for then accrued payments due under the Development Schedule, plus the prorated portion of the next payment, if any, due with respect to items being worked on but not yet delivered at the time of termination. The pro-rata payment shall be calculated by determining what percentage of the total work required for the next milestone has been completed by the date of Developer's receipt of the termination notice.

9.3 **Automatic Termination.** This Agreement will be terminated automatically, without notice, (i) upon the institution by or against Developer of insolvency, receivership, or bankruptcy proceedings or any other proceedings for the settlement of Developer's debts; (ii) upon Developer making an assignment for the benefit of creditors; or (iii) upon Developer's dissolution.

## Section 10
## GOVERNING LAW AND DISPUTE RESOLUTION

10.1 **Arbitration.** The parties agree to submit any dispute arising out of or in connection with this Agreement to binding arbitration in _____ before the American Arbitration Association pursuant to the provisions of this Section 10.1, and, to the extent not inconsistent with this Section 10.1, the rules of the American Arbitration Association. The parties agree that such arbitration will be in lieu of either party's rights to assert any claim, demand or suit in any court action, (provided that either party may elect either binding arbitration or a court action with respect to obtain injunctive relief to terminate the violation by the other party of such party's proprietary rights, including without limitation any trade secrets, copyrights or trademarks). Any arbitration shall be final and binding and the arbitrator's order will be enforceable in any court of competent jurisdiction.

10.2 **Governing Law; Venue.** The validity, construction, and performance of this Agreement shall be governed by the laws of the state of _____ , and all claims and/or lawsuits in connection with agreement must be brought in _____.

## Section 11
## MISCELLANEOUS PROVISIONS

11.1 **Notices.** For purposes of all notices and other communi cations required or permitted to be given hereunder, the addresses of the parties hereto shall be as indicated below. All notices shall be in writing and shall be deemed to have been duly given if sent by facsimile, the receipt of which is confirmed by return facsimile, or sent by first class registered or certified mail or equivalent, return receipt requested, addressed to the parties at their addresses set forth below:

If to Developer:

_____

_____

_____

Attn: _____

If to Client:

_____

_____

_____

Attn: _____

11.2 **Designated Person.** The parties agree that all materials exchanged between the parties for formal approval shall be communicated between single designated persons, or a single alternate designated person for each party. Neither party shall have any obligation to consider for approval or respond to materials submitted other than through the Designated Persons. Each party shall have the right to change its Designated Persons from time to time and to so notify the other in writing of such change. The initial Designated Person for Client is _____ and for Developer is _____ .

11.3 **Entire Agreement.** This Agreement, including the attached Schedules which are incorporated herein by reference as though fully set out, contains the entire understanding and agreement of the parties with respect to the subject matter contained herein, supersedes all prior oral or written understandings and agreements relating thereto except as expressly otherwise provided, and may not be altered, modified or waived in whole or in part, except in writing, signed by duly authorized representatives of the parties.

11.4 **Force Majeure.** Neither party shall be held responsible for damages caused by any delay or default due to any contingency beyond its control preventing or interfering with performance hereunder.

11.5 **Severability.** If any provision of this Agreement shall be held by a court of competent jurisdiction to be contrary to any law, the remaining provisions shall remain in full force and effect as if said provision never existed.

11.6 **Assignment.** This Agreement is personal to Developer. Developer may not sell, transfer, sublicense, hypothecate or assign its rights and duties under this Agreement without the written consent of Client. No rights of Developer hereunder shall devolve by operation of law or otherwise upon any receiver, liquidator, trustee, or other party. This Agreement shall inure to the benefit of Client, its successors and assigns.

11.7 **Waiver and Amendments.** No waiver, amendment, or modification of any provision of this Agreement shall be effective unless consented to by both parties in writing. No failure or delay by either party in exercising any rights, power, or remedy under this Agreement shall operate as a waiver of any such right, power, or remedy.

11.8 **Agency.** The parties are separate and independent legal entities. Developer is performing services for Client as an independent contractor. Nothing contained in this Agreement shall be deemed to constitute either Developer or Client an agent, representative, partner, joint venturer or employee of the other party for any purpose. Neither party has the authority to bind the other or to incur any liability on behalf of the other, nor to direct the employees of the other. Developer is an independent contractor, not an employee of Client. No employment relationship is created by this Agreement. Developer shall retain independent professional status throughout this Agreement and shall use his/her own discretion in performing the tasks assigned.

11.9 **Limitation on Liability; Remedies.** EXCEPT AS PROVIDED IN SECTION 8 ABOVE WITH RESPECT TO THIRD PARTY INDEMNIFICATION, NEITHER PARTY SHALL BE LIABLE TO THE OTHER PARTY FOR ANY INCIDENTAL, CONSEQUENTIAL, SPECIAL, OR PUNITIVE DAMAGES OF ANY KIND OR NATURE, INCLUDING, WITHOUT LIMITATION, THE BREACH OF THIS AGREEMENT OR ANY TERMINATION OF THIS AGREEMENT, WHETHER SUCH LIABILITY IS ASSERTED ON THE BASIS OF CONTRACT, TORT (INCLUDING NEGLIGENCE OR STRICT LIABILITY), OR OTHERWISE, EVEN IF EITHER PARTY HAS WARNED OR BEEN WARNED OF THE POSSIBILITY OF ANY SUCH LOSS OR DAMAGE.

IN WITNESS WHEREOF, this Agreement is executed as of the Effective Date set forth above.

[Client]

By: _____

Name

Its: _____

Title

[Developer]

By: _____

Name

Its: _____

Title

## SCHEDULE A
## SPECIFICATIONS (attach)

## SCHEDULE B
## DEVELOPMENT AND PAYMENT SCHEDULE

Contract Signing: _____     Payment due: _____

DELIVERABLES

|  | Due Date | Payment Due Upon | Acceptance by Client |
|---|---|---|---|
| Delivery of Web Site Design | | | |
| Delivery of Beta Version | | | |
| Delivery of Final Version /Source Materials | | | |

TOTAL PAYMENT:

**Bonus.** Client agrees to pay Developer a bonus of $_____ which shall be payable to Developer in the event Developer delivers a Final Version of the Web Site which is acceptable to Client prior to _____.

## SCHEDULE C
## CLIENT CONTENT

| ITEM | OWNER |
|---|---|

## SCHEDULE D
## MAINTENANCE AND SUPPORT SERVICES

## SCHEDULE E
## DEVELOPER'S CREDIT

# FORM 7

# Internet Advertising Contract

DO YOU WANT TO SELL ADVERTISING SPACE on your Web site to others? Or do you want to advertise your Web site on another company's Web site? If so, you need Form 7. If you are only agreeing to link to another Web site, you should use Form 11B.

This form is designed for the situation in which a Web site owner ("Host Provider") provides space for the ad of another party ("the Customer"), with a hypertext link (hotlink) in the ad to the Customer's own Web site.

The Host Provider's Web site is the "Host Site." The Customer's independent Web site is the "Advertised Site."

The form can be modified to cover other advertising transactions—for example, one in which the Customer's "banner" ad is linked to the Customer's full-page ad on the Host Site.

This agreement does not cover design or operation of the Customer's Advertised Site or design of the ad. Either the Advertised Site is already in existence, or it is to be

**Cross-References**

For a discussion of applicable laws for Form 7, see the following sections in the Overview: Copyright Law, Other Intellectual Property Laws, Contracts Law, Sales Law. For coverage of laws and regulations governing advertising and deceptive trade practices, consult your attorney or other publications.

developed by the Customer or by a Web site developer. The agreement does not cover Internet access for the Customer or server space for the Customer's Advertised Site.

## Checklist Of Issues

1. Will Customer's ad be linked to Customer's own Web site? Sections 2 and 3 assume this linkage. If Customer's ad is to be linked to another page on the Host Site, these sections must be revised. References to the Advertised Site must be deleted, and a description of the parties' obligations with respect to the full-page ad included.

2. What services will Host Provider provide with respect to Customer's advertisement (Section 3)? Four options are listed in this form: static display (display on the Host Site without rotation); random rotation display on the Host Site (display constantly rotated to different locations on the Host Site); targeted result display (display on Results Pages in response to Host Site visitor searches on specified keywords); and targeted page display (display on specified pages of the Host Site, such as the menu page or a page targeted to a particular market segment). Delete any of these selections that do not apply, and, if Host Provider is to provide different services—for example, rotation of several Customer ads through the same "banner"—add appropriate language.

3. If the advertisement is to be displayed in static display or random rotation display, what is the minimum number of impressions Host Provider will provide (Section 4)? And how is "impression" defined for the agreement? Is an impression counted every time the Web page containing the advertisement is loaded in front of a visitor to the Host Site, whether or not the visitor waits long enough for the whole page to load? Or must the visitor wait for the whole page to load for an impression to be counted? Different Web advertising providers use the term differently. Some providers use the term "page view" for the number of times a page is completely loaded and "impression" for any act of user loading, no matter how short or incomplete.

4. What is the advertising fee (Section 5)? The fee can take several forms: a monthly fee; a fee based on the number of monthly impressions (usually stated as a cost-per-thousand impressions); or a fee based on "clicks" (the number of Host Site visitors who click through from the advertisement on the Host Site to the Customer's Advertised Site, also known as "depressions" and "click-throughs"). Some host companies are now offering their customers results-based rates such as cost-per-sale or cost-per-action. For cost-per-sale, the Host Site would use Web ad management tools to monitor which Host Site visitors click on the ad and then buy the products advertised in the Customer's Advertised Site. Host Provider's fee

would be a percentage of the resulting sales revenue. If there are no sales, the ad is free. For "cost-per-action," the Host Site would get paid only for the number of Host Site users who take some specified action, such as filling out an electronic survey or requesting product information or samples.

5. What warranties will be given by Host Provider? As written, this form provides for a Host Provider warranty that it will make a reasonable effort to perform its services in a competent manner (Section 7). Host Provider may wish to limit its liability for any error in performance. The form limits Host Provider's liability to the amount of the advertising fees paid by Customer in the 12 months preceding the event giving rise to the claim of liability (Section 9).

6. What warranties will be given by Customer (Section 10)? As written, this form provides for a Customer warranty that the advertisement is truthful and will not violate any laws or regulations; that it will not infringe or misappropriate any third-party intellectual property rights or privacy/publicity rights; and that it does not contain any material that is unlawful, harmful, abusive, hateful, obscene, threatening, or defamatory. Because displaying an unlawful ad or one that violates third-party rights could expose Host Provider to liability, this provision includes an obligation by Customer to indemnify Host Provider.

7. What information will be included in the monthly reports to Customer (Section 11)? This information is designed to help Customer measure the effectiveness of the ad. The information could include daily and monthly impressions, page views, clicks, and click-rates. Click-rate—also known as click-through rates—is the number of clicks on the ad by visitors to the Host Site as a percentage of the number of times the ad page was loaded by visitors to the Host Site clicks (in other words, clicks divided by impressions or page views). Host Provider should be obligated to use a commercially reasonable (or agreed upon) means of obtaining this information (and this obligation is stated in Section 7's second sentence). In addition, Host Provider should take appropriate steps to ensure that the use of such information does not violate any rules relating to consumer privacy.

8. Who will sign the agreement? If an advertising agency is to sign the agreement on behalf of Customer, the agreement should include a representation and warranty by the ad agency that it is fully authorized to act as Customer's agent in signing the agreement on Customer's behalf and agrees to be fully liable for all amounts due under the agreement if the authorization is not valid or enforceable.

## Negotiating Tips: Host Provider

- **Services.** Many terms used in Internet advertising—"impressions" and "click," for example—do not have widely agreed definitions. You should define the terms you use.

- **Guaranteed Impressions.** If you are promising a minimum number of "impressions" and fail to provide the promised monthly minimum, Section 4's second sentence states that you will, without additional charge, extend the term of the contract until the minimum number of impressions is reached, and that such term extension will be Customer's sole remedy for breach of the guarantee.

- **Advertising Fee.** You may want to provide for a separate fee for setting up the advertisement and for changing the advertisement. If Customer wants a long-term contract, you might want to reserve the right to revise your rates on 30 days' written notice to Customer (but then Customer should have the right to terminate the agreement without penalty by notifying you in writing prior to the effective date of the revised rate).

- **Disclaimer of Article Two Implied Warranties.** Section 7 contains a disclaimer of the Uniform Commercial Code Article Two implied warranties, and Section 9 excludes Article Two buyer's remedies of incidental and consequential damages from this agreement. Technically, Article Two's provisions apply only to contracts for the sale of goods. However, many courts look to Article Two's provisions for guidance in cases involving other kinds of contracts. Article Two is discussed in the Sales Law section of the Overview.

## Negotiating Tips: Customer

- **Services.** You should make certain that you understand what services Host Provider is promising to provide. Ask for definitions of terms you don't understand and for any terms whose meaning may vary, such as "impression." If you don't understand Host Provider's terminology, get help.

- **Advertising Fee.** If you are not sure this sort of advertising will increase your sales revenues (or get you other results you want), you should try to negotiate for "results-based" rates (described in Item 4 of the checklist). If the fee is based on "click-throughs," the contract should include an obligation on the Hosting Site not to take action to artificially increase the number of click-throughs by action of Host Provider or its employees.

- **Duration of Agreement.** If you are uncertain whether this sort of advertising will work for you, you might also try to get a right to terminate the agreement upon 30 days' written notice to Host Provider. Or you could make the term of the agreement short.

# INTERNET ADVERTISING CONTRACT

This agreement ("Agreement") is hereby entered into between _____ ("Host Provider") and _____ ("Customer") on the _____ (the "Effective Date").

NOW, THEREFORE, in consideration of the promises and mutual covenants and agreements set forth herein, the parties agree as follows:

1. HOST PROVIDER'S BUSINESS.   Host Provider operates a site on the World Wide Web known as _____ (the "Host Site") located at http:// _____ . The Host Site contains Advertisements for third-party Web sites. An Advertisement is a graphical and text-based description of an advertised site with a hypertext pointer which, when clicked by a mouse, moves Host Site end users from the Host Site to the advertised site designated by the Customer ("Advertisement).

2. GENERAL UNDERTAKING.   Customer operates a site on the World Wide Web known as   (the "Advertised Site") located at http:// _____ . Customer wishes to place an Advertisement for Customer's Web Site on the Host Site. With this Agreement, Customer requests the Host Provider to provide the services stated in Section 3, and Host Provider agrees to provide those services, for a term of _____ beginning on _____ , 199 ___.

3. SERVICES.   Host Provider agrees to provide the following services:

   (a) Static Display. The Advertisement will be displayed without rotation on the Host Site.

   (b) Random Display. The Advertisement will be displayed on the Host Site in random rotation such that at least _____ impressions are delivered in each calendar month.

   (c) Targeted Result Display. Customer's Advertisement will be displayed on Result Pages in response to searches by end users to the Host Site on the KEYWORDS _____.

   (d) Targeted Page Display. The Advertisement will be displayed on the following specific pages of the Host Site: _____. The contents of the Targeted Display Page shall remain similar to the contents on the Effective Date.

4. MINIMUM IMPRESSIONS.   If the Advertisement is displayed in Static Display or Random Display, the Host Provider will make reasonable business efforts to display the Minimum Monthly Impressions per month. For the purpose of this Agreement, an "impression" is defined as follows: _____. If the Minimum Monthly Impressions are not reached in any calendar month, the sole remedy of Customer shall be to have the Host Provider extend the term of the Agreement at no additional charge to Customer until the Advertisement receives the total number of Impressions promised (calculated by multiplying the number of months in the initial term of the Agreement by the Minimum Monthly Impressions). For Targeted Results and Targeted Page display, there is no guarantee as to the number of impressions that will be displayed.

5. ADVERTISING FEE.   For the services described in Section 3, Customer agrees to pay Host Provider a fee of _____ plus any applicable state and local taxes. The fee is payable each month upon receipt of invoice. Delinquent accounts are subject to monthly interest and service charges at a rate of _____ per month (_____ per

annum), or the maximum allowed by law, plus collection costs (including, without limitation, reasonable attorneys' fees), until paid in full.

Host Provider reserves the right to suspend further display of the Advertisement or cancel this Agreement on ten (10) days written notice to Customer if Customer fails to pay any amount when due.

6. ADVERTISEMENT. Customer will submit its Advertisement to the Host Provider by _____, 199 \_\_\_, in the format specified in Exhibit A (Advertising Submission Specifications).

Host Provider may, in its sole judgment, reject any Advertisement which does not meet the specifications stated in Exhibit A, and it reserves the right to reject or terminate the display of an Advertisement if it fails to conform to applicable laws and regulations, Host Site's policies, or the public interest. Host Provider may reject or remove an Advertisement for an Advertised Site which is not functional or which Host Provider deems unsuitable for linking to the Host Site. If Host Provider rejects Customer's Advertisement or terminates its display, then this Agreement shall be deemed terminated, and Host Provider will return any prepaid advertising fees to Customer (in which case refund of those fees shall be Customer's sole remedy for the termination of this Agreement).

7. HOST PROVIDER'S OBLIGATIONS. The Host Provider shall use reasonable commercial efforts to maintain the Host Site available and display the Advertising twenty four hours per day each day during the term of the Agreement. The Host Provider shall install and maintain a commercially acceptable system of collecting information about Impressions and other data relating to the use of the Advertisement. Host Provider warrants to Customer that it will make a reasonable effort to perform its services under this Agreement in a competent manner. Host Provider does not warrant that it will be able to correct all reported defects or that use of the Host Site, Advertisement, or that the hypertext pointer to the Advertised Site will be uninterrupted or error-free. Host Provider makes no warranty regarding features or services provided by third parties. HOST PROVIDER DISCLAIMS ALL IMPLIED WARRANTIES, INCLUDING WITHOUT LIMITATION, THE WARRANTIES OF MERCHANTABILITY, NON-INFRINGEMENT OF THIRD PARTY RIGHTS, AND FITNESS FOR A PARTICULAR PURPOSE. The Host Provider reserves the right, in its sole discretion, to determine all matters concerning hardware and software selection and configuration, telecommunications, system components, advertising categories, positioning of Customer's Advertisement (except for Targeted Page Display), and other operational and administrative matters for the Host Site.

8. INTELLECTUAL PROPERTY RIGHTS.

a. Each party to this Agreement owns its respective Web site and the material and content on its Web site. Except as stated in Section 8(b), nothing in this Agreement grants to one party any right, title, or license to the other party's intellectual property rights.

b. Customer grants Host Provider a nonexclusive license to set up and display the Customer's Advertisement (including any trademarks and service marks shown) and to hyperlink to the Advertised Site during the Term of this Agreement. Upon termination of this Agreement, the Host Provider will uninstall the Customer's Advertisement, destroy all copies of it, cease further display of the Advertisement, and terminate the hyperlink to Customer's Site.

c. Nothing in this Agreement grants Customer any right to use the name, trademark, or service mark of Host Provider in any advertisement, sales promotion or press release without Host Provider's prior written approval.

9. HOST PROVIDER'S LIABILITY. Customer agrees that Host Provider's liability for any error in displaying the Advertisement or any failure to provide services shall not exceed the Advertising Fees paid by Customer in the 12 months preceding the event giving rise to Customer's claim. If Host Provider is unable to display the Advertisement at any time during the term of this Agreement due to acts of God, war, riot, strikes, system or transmission failure, or for any other reason beyond its reasonable control, such failure to display the Advertisement will not constitute a breach of this Agreement; provided, however that Customer may terminate this Agreement if such failure to display the Advertisement continues for more than twenty (20) days. If such failure to display the Advertisement is caused by an act or omission of the Customer, Host Provider shall be entitled to full payment of all Advertising Fees. If such failure to display the Advertisement is not caused by an act or omission of the Customer, but a failure of Host Provider to meet its obligations, Host Provider will allow a pro rata reduction in the Advertising Fee. IN NO EVENT SHALL HOST PROVIDER BE LIABLE, WHETHER IN CONTRACT, TORT (INCLUDING NEGLIGENCE), OR OTHERWISE, FOR ANY INDIRECT, INCIDENTAL, OR CONSEQUENTIAL DAMAGES (INCLUDING LOST SALES OR PROFIT, LOST DATA, BUSINESS INTERRUPTION OR ATTORNEYS' FEES), EVEN IF NOTIFIED IN ADVANCE OF SUCH POSSIBILITY.

10. CUSTOMER'S WARRANTIES. The Customer warrants that the Advertisement:

    a. Is truthful and will not violate any foreign, federal, state or local law or regulation;

    b. Will not infringe or misappropriate any copyright, trademark, patent, trade secrets, publicity or privacy rights of any person or third-party in any jurisdiction;

    c. Does not contain any material which is unlawful, harmful, abusive, hateful, obscene, threatening, or defamatory.

    Customer agrees to defend, indemnify, and hold harmless Host Provider, its officers, directors, sublicensees, employees and agents, from and against any claims, actions or demands, including without limitation reasonable legal and accounting fees, alleging or resulting from the breach of the warranties in Section 10. Host Provider shall provide notice to Customer promptly of any such claim, suit, or proceeding and shall assist Customer, at Customer's expense, in defending any such claim, suit or proceeding.

11. REPORTS. Once a month during the term of this Agreement, the Host Provider will provide the Customer will provide the Customer with a written report showing _____. Customer shall have the right to use such data for its internal business purposes, but may not provide such data for use by third parties.

12. CHANGES TO ADVERTISEMENT. Customer or its agents may make changes to

the Advertisement no more often than _____. Changes must be in the format stated in Exhibit A. After changes have been received by the Host Site, Host Site will have business days to implement the changes.

14. TERMINATION.

(a) Except as provided below, this Agreement will terminate without further action upon the expiration of the period set forth in Section 2 unless extended as provided in Section 4 for failing to meet the Minimum Impressions per Month. This Agreement may be terminated by the non-breaching party upon thirty (30) days prior written notice upon the material breach of a provision of this Agreement; provided that if such breach is cured within such period, the Agreement shall continue in effect.

(b) Customer acknowledges that Host Provider may terminate this Agreement and remove the Advertisement if the Host Provider believes in its sole discretion that the Advertisement breaches any warranty. In the event of such termination, Host Provider shall be entitled to receive full payment for all Advertising Fees incurred by Customer up to the date of termination.

(c) This Agreement will be terminated automatically, without notice, (i) upon the institution by or against Host Provider of insolvency, receivership, or bankruptcy proceedings or any other proceedings for the settlement of Host Provider's debts; (ii) upon Host Provider making an assignment for the benefit of creditors; or (iii) upon Host Provider's dissolution.

15. GENERAL PROVISIONS. This Agreement will be governed by and construed in accordance with the laws of the United States and the State of  as applied to agreements entered into and to be performed entirely within that state between residents of that state. This Agreement, including any Exhibits to this Agreement, constitutes the entire agreement between the parties relating to this subject matter and supersedes all prior or simultaneous representations, discussions, negotiations, and agreements, whether written or oral. The Agreement may not be modified except by written instrument signed by both parties. No term or provision hereof will be considered waived by either party, and no breach excused by either party, unless such waiver or consent is in writing signed on behalf of the party against whom the waiver is asserted. No consent by either party to, or waiver of, a breach by either party, whether express or implied, will constitute a consent to, waiver of, or excuse of any other, different, or subsequent breach by either party. Customer may not assign its rights or obligations arising under this Agreement without Host Provider's prior written consent. Host Provider may assign its rights and obligations under this Agreement. This Agreement will be for the benefit of Host Provider's successors and assigns, and will be binding on Customer's heirs, legal representatives and permitted assignees. If any dispute arises between the parties with respect to the matters covered by this Agreement which leads to a proceeding to resolve such dispute, the prevailing party in such proceeding shall be entitled to receive its reasonable attorneys' fees, expert witness fees and out-of-pocket costs incurred in connection with such proceeding, in addition to any other relief to which it may be entitled. All notices, requests and other communications required to be given under this Agreement must be in writing, and must be mailed by registered or certified mail,

postage prepaid and return receipt requested, or delivered by hand to the party to whom such notice is required or permitted to be given. Any such notice will be considered to have been given when received, or if mailed, five (5) business days after it was mailed, as evidenced by the postmark. The mailing address for notice to either party will be the address shown on the signature page of this Agreement. Either party may change its mailing address by notice as provided by this Section. The following provisions shall survive termination of this Agreement: Sections 9, 10, and the right to use data in 11.

This Agreement is effective as of _____, 19_____ .

By: _____    By: _____

_____        _____
Typed name                              Typed name

_____        _____
Title                                   Title

_____        _____

_____        _____
Address:                                Address:

# EXHIBIT A

## Advertising Submission Specifications

# FORM 8

# Chat Room Agreement

DOES YOUR WEB SITE OFFER A CHAT FUNCTION (real-time conversation) or include a bulletin board? If so, you may be liable for copyright infringement, defamation, and other wrongs committed by users. You need Form 8.

The purpose of Form 8 is to state rules for the Chat Room or bulletin board. These rules prohibit the use of the Chat Room for illegal purposes and the posting of material which infringes or violates the rights of others. And they make it clear that certain kinds of conduct are not permitted.

The scope of liability for a Chat Room provider is still an open question. For example:

- If a Chat Room user posts part of a book for which he does not own the copyright, the Chat Room provider could be liable for "contributory copyright infringement."

- If a Chat Room provider monitors user postings carefully and a user libels an individual, the Chat Room provider could be liable as a "publisher" (although the scope of such liability in the United States has been dramatically reduced by a provision of

**Cross-References**

For a discussion of the applicable laws for Form 8, see the following sections in the Overview: Copyright Law, Other Intellectual Property Laws, Privacy and Defamation Law, Contracts Law.

the Communications Decency Act, as discussed in the Overview section Privacy and Defamation Law).

Using this form will not prevent you from being sued—for example, by a copyright owner whose material is posted without permission by a Chat Room user. However, it will help you establish that you should not be held liable for the user's wrongful act. And it will remind users not to post material that might get them (and you) in trouble—hopefully, keeping "problem" material to a minimum.

For additional protection, you may want to try to obtain indemnities from users of your Chat Room that they will hold you harmless if they violate the Chat Room Agreement and you get sued. However, such indemnities are of limited value when given by users with limited assets (and requiring them may discourage people from using your Chat Room). This form does not include an indemnity for those reasons, but you can revise the indemnity in Section 8 of Form 4 for this purpose.

For this form, there are no issues to be negotiated—you're providing the Chat Room facilities, and the users must accept your rules.

Technically, Form 8 is a contract between you, the Web site operator/Chat Room provider, and a user. But how do you get a user to express assent to your terms? From a legal point of view, the best way to do this is to: (1) put the information in this form on a "terms of usage" screen which a user must pass through before entering the Chat Room; (2) make the user do something to show assent to the terms before entering the Chat Room—for example, by registering and typing "I agree"; (3) keep records of the user assents; and (4) give users the option of exiting at the "terms" screen if they do not want to accept those rules.

Does that sound like too much trouble? Many Chat Room providers simply state at the bottom of the "terms" screen that entering the Chat Room represents the user's assent to the stated terms. If you choose this approach, it's best to require users to click through the "terms" screen in order to chat (don't just bury the "terms" screen somewhere on your Web site).

If you intend to use postings from the Chat Room users for your own purposes, you will need a license for such use. The copyright in a user's posting is owned by the user (or his employer, if the posting is a work for hire). A license is included in this agreement (Section 3a).

In this agreement, the Web site owner/Chat Room provider is referred to as "Company." The user is referred to as "User."

# CHAT ROOM AGREEMENT

SECTION 1. WEB SITE OWNER'S RIGHTS AND DUTIES

As a Chat Room User ("User"), you are responsible for your own communications and are responsible for the consequences of posting those communications.

("Company") does not represent or guarantee the truthfulness, accuracy, or reliability of any of material posted by Chat Room Users or endorse any opinions expressed by Users. User acknowledges that any reliance on material posted by other Users will be at User's own risk.

Company does not screen communications in advance and is not responsible for screening or monitoring material posted by Users. If notified by a User of communications which allegedly do not conform to this Chat Room Agreement, Company may investigate the allegation and determine in good faith and its sole discretion whether to remove or request the removal of the communication. Company has no liability or responsibility to Users for performance or nonperformance of such activities.

Company reserves the right to expel Users and prevent their further access to the Chat Room for violating the Chat Room Agreement or the law and the right to remove communications which are abusive, illegal, or disruptive.

SECTION 2. USER AGREEMENT.

In consideration of being allowed to use the Chat Room facilities provided by Company, User agrees that User will not:

a. Use the Chat Room facilities for any purpose in violation of local, state, or national laws of any country.

b. Post material that is copyrighted, unless User is the copyright owner or has the permission of the copyright owner to post it.

c. Post material that reveals trade secrets, unless User owns them or has the permission of the copyright owner.

d. Post material that infringes on any other intellectual property rights of others or on the privacy or publicity rights of others.

e. Post material that is obscene, defamatory, threatening, harassing, abusive, hateful, or embarrassing to another User or any other person or entity.

f. Post sexually-explicit images.

g. Post advertisements or solicitations of business.

h. Disrupt the normal flow of dialogue, or post comments that are not related to the topic being discussed (unless it is clear that the discussion is free-form).

i. Post chain letters or pyramid schemes.

j. Impersonate another person.

SECTION 3. LICENSE.

By posting communications, User grants:

a. To Company: A royalty-free, perpetual, irrevocable nonexclusive license to use, reproduce, modify, publish, translate, distribute, perform and display those communications alone or as part of other works in any form, media, or technology whether now known or hereafter developed and sublicense such rights through multiple tiers of sublicensees.

b. To other Users: The right to access, view, store, and reproduce the communications for personal use.

# FORM 9

# Internet Use Policy

DO YOU HAVE EMPLOYEES who use your computers and telecommunications equipment to access the Internet and send email? If so, you need Form 9 for three reasons:

- An employer can be liable when an employee uses the employer's Internet access and intranet facilities to infringe third-party rights, harass, threaten, or for further unlawful purposes. By providing a clear Internet Use Policy, you will provide guidance to your employees and reduce inappropriate employee Internet uses—uses that might expose you, the employer, to liability.

- If you have an Internet Use Policy and an employee does something prohibited by the policy—for example, transmits copyrighted software without the permission of the copyright owner, or uses the company email system to sexually harass another employee—you may reduce your liability as an employer for that employee's unpermitted activities.

- If you do email and Internet-use monitoring of your employees, you should inform your employees of this monitoring and get their consent to protect yourself from breach of privacy claims by the employees.

**Cross-References**

For a discussion of the applicable laws for Form 9, see the following sections in the Overview: Copyright Law, Privacy and Defamation Law.

This policy makes it clear to employees that the computers and telecommunications equipment (called "Facilities" in the form) belong to the employer and are to be used for work-related purposes only (not for downloading images from *Playboy* or playing games).

This policy can be revised to define acceptable Internet use for schools, universities, and other organizations providing Internet access.

# INTERNET USE POLICY

This policy establishes guidelines for proper use of the computers, software, and telecommunications system of _____ ("Employer").

**Ownership of Facilities.** The computers, software and telecommunications system ("Facilities") belong to the Employer. Employees are given access to the Internet and to the Facilities to help them perform their job duties and further Employer's interests.

**Use of Facilities.** Except for occasional personal use, the Facilities are to be used for authorized business purposes only. Employer will determine in its sole discretion the scope of permissible "occasional personal use".

Access. Employees may access the Internet only through an approved Internet firewall. Direct access by modem is strictly prohibited unless the accessing computer is not connected to the Employer's network.

**Prohibited Use.** Employees may not use the Facilities for commercial advertisements, solicitations, or promotions other than on behalf of the Employer and to further the Employer's interests; for personal advertisements, solicitations, or promotions; for the dissemination of destructive programs such as virus software and self-replicating code; for the dissemination of political material; or for any other unauthorized use.

**Prohibited Activities.** Use of the Facilities to further any unlawful purpose is prohibited. Transmitting, receiving, displaying, printing, forwarding, or otherwise disseminating material that is fraudulent, illegal, harassing, offensive, embarrassing, sexually explicit, obscene, threatening, or defamatory is prohibited.

**Codes.** Access codes must be disclosed to the Employer. The use of unauthorized codes or passwords to gain access to files on the Facilities is prohibited.

**Trade secrets disclosure.** Employer's trade secrets/confidentiality policy applies to the Internet and the Facilities. In communicating with others, exercise at least the same level of care in what you reveal as you do when using other forms of communication. The Internet is not a secure medium unless encryption or other similar measures are taken. Sensitive or confidential information should not be communicated over the Internet unless security safeguards are in place.

**Commitments on Behalf of Employer.** Statements made in emails can bind Employer. Employees should use the same level of care in email messages that they use in other forms of communication. In particular, Employees should not make negative statements about the products of third parties.

**Viruses.** All material downloaded from the Internet or from computers or networks that do not belong to the Employer must be scanned for viruses before being placed onto the Facilities.

**Waiver of Privacy.** Employer has the right but not the duty to monitor any and all aspects of its computer system, including, but not limited to, reviewing email sent and received by employees; monitoring chat rooms and newsgroups; reviewing material downloaded or uploaded by employees; and monitoring Web sites visited by employees. Employee, by signing this Policy, acknowledges that email messages sent or received using the Facilities are business messages which belong to the Employer, and not personal, confidential information belonging to the Employee.

**Intellectual Property Laws.** Employees using the Facilities must respect and avoid infringing the intellectual property rights of others, including but not limited to copyrights, trademark rights, patent rights, trade secret rights, and publicity and privacy rights. Copying material from Web sites without permission may be copyright infringement. Use of the Facilities to violate third-party intellectual property rights is strictly prohibited.

**Sexual Harassment and Non-Discrimination Policy.** Employer's policy prohibiting sexual harassment and discrimination applies to the Internet and the Facilities.

I have read this Policy and agree to comply with it. I understand that violation of this Policy may result in disciplinary action, including possible termination and legal action.

Signed: _____

Printed Name: _____

Date: _____

# FORM 10

# Clickwrap Agreement

ARE YOU LICENSING SOFTWARE OR SELLING GOODS on your Web site? If so, you need Form 10, a "Clickwrap."

Form 10 can be used to define the terms and conditions of a sale or license, to disclaim implied warranties of merchantability and fitness, and to limit liability. It can be used whether delivery of the goods or software takes place online or off-line (by mail or a package delivery company). If you want to inform users of your Web site of the terms under which they may use the Web site and what use they may make of Web site materials, use Form 4.

This form assumes that separate screens on the Web site deal with what the customer is buying or licensing, the price or license fee, and the payment terms and mechanism.

In this form, the buyer/licensee is referred to as "You." The seller/licensor is "Company." The subject matter of the agreement—what the customer is buying or licensing—is referred to as "the Product."

As written, Form 10 is a clickwrap for the licensing of software. The form can easily be modified to use for the sale of goods.

**Cross-References**

For a discussion of the applicable laws for Form 10, see the following sections in the Overview: Copyright Law, Copyright Licenses, Contracts Law, and Sales Law.

## Checklist Of Issues For Seller/Licensor

1. The purpose of the procedure described in the first paragraph, above Section 1, is to establish that the buyer/licensee has actively manifested "assent" after having had an opportunity to review the terms of the agreement. It is unclear under current United States law whether clickwraps are enforceable without proof that the buyer/licensee read and assented to the terms. By following this procedure, you will improve your chances of being able to enforce the agreement. This topic is discussed in more detail in "Sales Law" in the Overview.

2. If your Product is software or other material protected by copyright and other intellectual property laws, you may want to use Section 2 to define permitted and prohibited uses of the Product. We've included a typical provision for the license of software for use on a single computer. Modify Section 2 as necessary to fit your needs.

3. What warranty are you giving? This information goes in Section 3. There are many options. For example, for software, you could warrant that the Product will perform substantially in accordance with the performance specifications stated on another screen on the Web site for a limited period of time. Or you could warrant that the software will perform substantially in accordance with the accompanying documentation for 90 days after delivery to the customer. For goods, you could warrant that the Product is free of manufacturing defects. You also may choose to make no warranty as to performance, stating instead that you are providing the Product on "as is" basis, with the user assuming the entire risk of using the Product.

4. If you are selling "goods" as defined in the Uniform Commercial Code (see "Sales Law"), implied warranties are part of the sales contract unless you disclaim them. Section 4 is a disclaimer, which must be "conspicuous" (that's why Section 4 is in capital letters). This disclaimer language is designed for United States law and may not be valid in other countries. It is not valid even in the United States for certain warranties on "consumer products" (see "Sales Law"). This agreement has been drafted for consumer products. If you are only selling products to businesses, delete the last two sentences in Section 4 and the last sentence in Section 6.

5. If you are selling "goods" as defined in the Uniform Commercial Code, a buyer will be entitled to collect consequential damages from you for breach unless you exclude these damages. Consequential damages are any loss that could not reasonably be prevented by the buyer that resulted from the buyer's requirements and needs that the seller knew about or had reason to know about. Most manufacturers and sellers try to exclude consequential damages because such

liability exposes a seller to a risk of having to pay damages far in excess of the product's price. Section 6 excludes consequential damages.

6. Federal law provides that when software is licensed for U.S. Government use, the government users get special "default" rights in the software unless the software is expressly provided pursuant to government "Commercial Software" regulations, which permit the licensor to restrict those rights. Section 10 includes the necessary provisions to restrict the rights, but you should ensure that the references in the provision to government regulations are still correct when you start distributing your software. If you are distributing other types of material, you should check to determine if other special rules for U.S. Government users apply.

## CLICKWRAP AGREEMENT

PLEASE READ THIS AGREEMENT CAREFULLY. TO COMPLETE YOUR ORDER FOR THE PRODUCT YOU'VE REQUESTED, YOU MUST FIRST ACCEPT THE TERMS AND CONDITIONS OF THIS AGREEMENT BY ELECTRONICALLY CHECKING THE BOX MARKED "I ACCEPT THESE TERMS AND CONDITIONS."

**Section 1. Intellectual Property Rights.** The Product is protected by copyright and other intellectual property laws, and all intellectual property rights in the Product belong to the Company. You may not reproduce, publish, transmit, modify, create derivative works from, publicly display, or publicly perform the Product. Copying or storing the Product other than as permitted in Section 2 is expressly prohibited unless you obtain prior written permission from Company.

**Section 2. Permitted and Prohibited Uses.** You may use the Product on a single computer for your personal use or for the internal business use of your company. You may make a single copy of the Product for archival purposes and may use such copy only when the original copy is not in use. You may not use the Product on a computer network or allow concurrent use of the Product by more than one individual. You may not rent, lease or otherwise transfer the Product. Unless permitted by law, you may not reverse engineer, decompile, or disassemble the Product.

**Section 3. Limited Warranty.** Company warrants to the original purchaser or licensee that the Product _____. This Limited Warranty applies only if the nonconformance is reported to Company during the Warranty Period. It is void if the failure of the Product is the result of accident, abuse, misapplication, or inappropriate use of the Product.

**Section 4. No Other Warranties.** TO THE EXTENT PERMITTED BY LAW, COMPANY DISCLAIMS ALL OTHER WARRANTIES ON THE PRODUCT, EITHER EXPRESS OR IMPLIED, INCLUDING BUT NOT LIMITED TO THE IMPLIED WARRANTIES OF MERCHANTABILITY, NON-INFRINGEMENT OF THIRD PARTY RIGHTS, AND FITNESS FOR PARTICULAR PURPOSE. THE DURATION OF ANY STATUTORILY-REQUIRED WARRANTY PERIOD SHALL BE LIMITED TO THE TERM OF THE LIMITED WARRANTY. THIS LIMITED WARRANTY GIVES YOU SPECIFIC LEGAL RIGHTS, DEPENDING UPON WHERE YOU LIVE. YOU MAY HAVE OTHER RIGHTS, WHICH VARY FROM STATE TO STATE AND COUNTRY TO COUNTRY.

**Section 5. Exclusive Remedy.** The exclusive remedy for breach of this Agreement shall be, at Company's option, either (a) the repair or replacement of the Product that does not meet Company's Limited Warranty (and is returned with proof of license); or (b) a refund of the price, if any, which you paid to license the Product.

**Section 6. Disclaimer of Consequential Damages.** UNDER NO CIRCUMSTANCES SHALL COMPANY BE LIABLE FOR ANY CONSEQUENTIAL OR INCIDENTAL DAMAGES WHATSOEVER ARISING OUT OF THE USE OF THE PRODUCT OR INABILITY TO USE THE PRODUCT, INCLUDING WITHOUT LIMITATION, COMPUTER FAILURE, WORK STOPPAGE OR ANY OTHER DAMAGES, EVEN IF COMPANY HAS BEEN ADVISED OF THE POSSIBILITY OF SUCH DAMAGES. BECAUSE SOME STATES AND COUNTRIES DO NOT ALLOW THE EXCLUSION OR LIMITATION OF LIABILITY FOR CONSEQUENTIAL OR INCIDENTAL DAMAGES, THE ABOVE LIMITATION MAY NOT APPLY TO YOU.

**Section 7. Limitation on Liability.** COMPANY'S LIABILITY SHALL IN NO EVENT EXCEED THE ACTUAL PRICE PAID FOR THE PRODUCT.

**Section 8. Export Control.** The United States controls the export of products and information. You agree to comply with such restrictions and not to export or re-export the Product to countries or persons prohibited under the export control laws. By downloading the Product, you are agreeing that you are not in a country where such export is prohibited or are a person or entity to which such export is prohibited. You are responsible for compliance with the laws of your local jurisdiction regarding the import, export or re-export of the Product.

**Section 9. Taxes.** You shall be responsible for the payment of all sales, use and similar taxes relating to the license of the Product.

**Section 10. Government Users.** If the Product is downloaded by or on behalf of the United States of America, its agencies and/or instrumentalities ("U.S. Government"), it is provided with Restricted Rights. Use, duplication, or disclosure of the Product by the U.S. Government is subject to restrictions as set forth in subparagraph (c)(1)(ii) of the Rights in Technical Data and Computer Software clause of DFARS 252-227-7013 or subparagraphs (c)(1) an d(2) of the Commercial Computer Software-Restricted Rights at 48 CFR 52.227-19, as applicable.

**Section 11. General Terms.** This agreement is governed by the laws of the State of _____. If any provision of this agreement is found to be invalid by any court having competent jurisdiction, the invalidity of such provision shall not affect the validity of the remaining provisions of this agreement, which shall remain in full force and effect. No waiver of any term of this agreement shall be deemed a further or continuing waiver of such term or any other term. This agreement constitutes the entire agreement between you and the Company with respect to this transaction. Any changes to this agreement must be made in writing, signed by an authorized representative of the Company.

# FORM 11

# Linking Agreements

DO YOU WANT TO PROVIDE A LINK from your Web site to another Web site? If so, we recommend that you get permission from the owner of the site to which you want to link. You can use Form 11A, Permission to Link.

If the owner of another Web site has asked you for permission to link to your site, use Form 11A to grant permission, setting restrictions and getting reciprocal permission, if you wish.

For situations in which a linked site is to share advertising revenues with a linking site, use Form 11B, Linking Agreement.

Web site links permit Web users to click their way from one Web site to another. Currently, linking can take three forms:

- A simple text hyperlink, implemented through HTML, in which a hypertext link is marked as a highlighted word or different-colored word on the linking site.
- A graphic hyperlink, in which a graphic (a trademarked logo or just a button) on the linking site alerts the user of the linking site to the existence of a link.

**Cross-References**

For a discussion of the applicable laws for Form 11, see the following sections in the Overview: Copyright Law, Copyright Ownership, Copyright Licenses, Other Intellectual Property Laws, and Contracts Law.

- "Framing," which permits a Web site user to view material from another Web site within a "frame" on the original site.

Other types of links may become possible as new technology becomes available.

Linking is so common on the World Wide Web that the idea that a Web site owner might need permission to link to another site was once considered absurd. In the Web culture, providing a link to another site generally has been viewed as a favor to the owner of the linked sites, because providing a link to the other site increases traffic to that site.

Lately, however, the increasing commercialization of the World Wide Web and the availability of new technology (such as framing technology) have caused the assumption that linking does not require permission to be reexamined, especially in light of two recent lawsuits over linking—Ticketmaster's suit against Microsoft for linking Microsoft's Sidewalk Seattle site to the ticket ordering section of the Ticketmaster site without permission; and the suit filed by *The Washington Post, The Wall Street Journal,* and several other publishers against TotalNEWS for using a framing link to their sites. The publisher plaintiffs in the TotalNEWS case were unhappy because the TotalNEWS site's "frame" covered up the original advertising from the framed sites (TotalNEWS sold its own advertising). The TotalNEWS case was settled recently, with the publishers granting TotalNEWS a limited right to create non-framing links to the plaintiffs' sites.

Currently, whether a Web site owner who wants to provide a link to another site must get permission from the owner of the linked site is open to debate. Linking without framing does not involve copying or displaying the linked site's pages, so it does not raise copyright infringement concerns (although framing may raise copyright issues). However, some Web site owners may not want to be associated with your site or your products. For this reason, we recommend that you use Form 11A and get permission before you provide a link from your Web site to another site.

Linking agreements can do more than grant permission for linking, however: They can promote commercial objectives such as a revenue-sharing arrangement between the owners of the linking and linked sites. In a revenue-sharing linking arrangement, the linking site's owner receives—as compensation for providing text or graphic image link to a another site—a percentage of the linked site's revenues (which come from product sales or advertising fees).

Form 11B is a revenue-sharing linking agreement. It is designed for the situation in which the linked Web site sells advertising space. The linking site's owner agrees to place a graphic image link on the linking site to "drive" linking site users to the linked site. In return, the linking site's owner receives a percentage of the ad revenues from the linked site.

# Form 11A Permission To Link

Use Form A to:

■ Get permission *from* another Web site owner to link from your site to the owner's site.

■ Grant permission *to* another Web site owner for your site to be linked to the owner's site.

In Form 11A, the party granting permission is the "Grantor." The party receiving permission is the "Grantee."

# Checklist Of Issues

1. Does Grantee want to use a graphic link rather than a hypertext link? If so, modify the third sentence.

2. If Grantee wants to use a graphic that belongs to Grantor as the link—Grantor's logo, for example—and Grantor is willing to grant Grantee permission to use the graphic, add this provision and attach an Exhibit showing the graphic (the "Grantor's Image"):

   "Grantor grants to Grantee a nonexclusive, worldwide license to reproduce and publicly display the Grantor's Image shown on Exhibit A on Grantee's Web site solely for the purpose of serving as a graphic image link to Grantor's Web site."

   If Grantor wants to specify how the Grantor's Image must appear to users of Grantee's Web site, modify Section 2.1 of Form 11B. Grantee should recognize that the use of the Grantor's Image on Grantee's Web site could infringe a third party's copyright rights, trademark rights, or other rights, exposing Grantee to liability to the third party.

3. Does Grantor want to specify where the link must be placed on Grantee's site? If so, add a provision stating where the link is to placed on Grantee's site.

4. The third sentence states that the link must go from Grantee's site to Grantor's home page. If the link is to go to another page of Grantor's Web site, modify this sentence.

5. Fill in a description of the manner in which termination notice must be given. For example, must the notice be given by certified letter? By regular mail? By email?

6. If Grantor sends a termination notice to Grantee, how long will Grantee have to remove the link? Fill in this information.

## PERMISSION TO LINK

_____ ("Grantor") has a Web site located at http://_____ ("Grantor's Web site").

_____ ("Grantee") has a Web site located at http://_____ ("Grantee's Web site").

Grantor hereby grants Grantee permission to provide a hypertext link from Grantee's Web site to the home page of Grantor's Web site.

Neither party shall be liable to the other party for the content of its Web site or links on its Web site to other Web sites.

Grantee acknowledges that Grantor may terminate this Permission at any time with or without cause by giving notice to Grantee in the following manner: _____.

If this Grant is terminated, Grantee must remove the hypertext link to Grantee's Web site within _____ days of receiving the notice.

This Agreement is governed by the laws of the State of _____, excluding its conflict of laws principles. This Agreement is the entire understanding between the parties relating to the link referenced here and supersedes all prior or contemporaneous understandings, whether written or oral.

# Form 11B Linking Agreement (Revenue-sharing)

Form 11B is a revenue-sharing linking agreement. The linking site's owner agrees to place a graphic image link on the linking site to "drive" linking site users to the linked site. In return, the linking site's owner receives a percentage of the ad revenues (or product sales revenue) from the linked site. It is designed for the situation in which the linked Web site sells advertising space. It can be revised to cover the situation in which the linked site sells products.

The linking Web site—the Web site providing a graphic link to the second site—is referred to as the "Licensor's Site" and is operated by "Licensor." The linked Web site is referred to as the "Licensee's Site" and is operated by "Licensee."

The graphic image used to alert users of the Licensor's Web site to the link's existence is called the "Licensee's Image." The Licensee's Image is placed on the Licensor's home page, to provide a link to Licensee's home page. When a user of Licensor's Site clicks on the Licensee's Image, the user is moved to Licensee's Site.

Form 11B assumes a one-way link (from Licensor's Web site to Licensee's Web site). It can be revised to add a link going the other way as well (from Licensee's Web site to Licensor's Web site).

## Checklist Of Issues

1. What type of link will Licensor provide on Licensor's Site? The agreement provides for a graphic image link (Sections 1.4 and 2.1). If a simple hypertext link or a framing link is to be used, revise these provisions.

2. Should the contract prohibit Licensor from providing links to the sites of Licensee's competitors? If Licensee is sharing revenues from Licensee's Site as compensation for the link, Licensee may expect such exclusivity.

3. Form 11B assumes that Licensor will receive a percentage of the advertising revenues from Licensee's Web site. If Licensor is to receive other compensation or only the compensation of a reciprocal link, revise the preamble (and the payment provisions, which are discussed below).

4. Where will the link be placed on Licensor's Web site? Section 2.1 states that Licensee's Image will be placed on Licensor's home page. Revise this section if different placement is chosen.

5. What are the requirements for the Licensee's Image's appearance and visibility to users of Licensor's Web site? Section 2.1 states specific requirements, which include the requirement that the Licensee's Image be visible at a certain size when

the Web site user first loads Licensor's home page. Revise these requirements as necessary.

6. What information must the parties give each other about users of their respective sites? Will Licensor have to share data about all users of Licensor's Site, or only about users who click through to Licensee's Site? Section 2.2 uses the second option. Will Licensee have to share data about all users on Licensee's Site, or only those users who get there from Licensor's Site? Section 3.2 uses the second option.

7. Should each party be required to ensure that the collection of such information is collected in accordance with various countries' privacy laws and regulations? This information can be valuable, and yet the rules regarding the collection and use of this information vary from country to country. Sections 2.2 and 3.2 require that Web site users be informed that the information being collected may be disclosed and used by other parties in the manner required by the most restrictive laws relating to the use of such personal information in major commercial countries: the United States, the countries of the European Union, Japan, Canada, and Australia.

8. Where will the link be placed on Licensee's Web site? Section 3.1 states that the link from the Licensee's Image on Licensor's Site will be placed by Licensee on Licensee's home page. Revise this section if different placement is chosen.

9. Will Licensee have the right to control the content of Licensor's Site? Section 2.3 gives Licensee the right to terminate the agreement if Licensor materially alters the content or structure of Licensor's Site.

10. How much control will Licensor have over the content of Licensee's Site? Section 3.3 gives Licensor the right to terminate the agreement if Licensee materially alters the content or structure of Licensee's Site.

11. Will Licensor have any control over what links Licensee's Site provides to third-party sites? Section 3.6(b) requires that existing links be stated on Exhibit B and that Licensor be notified of other Web sites which become linked to Licensee's Site during the term of the agreement.

12. How will Licensor's compensation be determined? Section 4.1 states that Licensee agrees to pay Licensor a dollar amount calculated by multiplying advertising revenue for Licensee's Site by "Licensor's AR Share." In Section 1.8, "Licensor's AR Share" is defined as the number of impressions on Licensee's Site by users who arrive through the link divided by the total number of impressions on Licensee's Site. "Impression" is defined in Section 1.2. Revise Section 4.1 if compensation is to be determined differently, defining any Web marketing terms which do not have widely accepted definitions and making certain that Web marketing tools are available to measure any site use criteria used in the agreement.

13. If Licensee's Site infringes the copyright or other rights of a third party, it is unclear whether Licensor will be liable to the third party. What protection, if any, will Licensor have against claims by third parties? This agreement deals with this issue by having Licensee give a warranty (Section 3.4) and an indemnity (Section 3.7) to Licensor.

14. Similarly, if Licensor's Site infringes the copyright or other rights of a third party, it is unclear whether Licensee will be liable to the third party. What protection, if any, will Licensee have against claims by the owners of those rights? Licensor's warranty of noninfringement is in Section 2.4, and Licensor's indemnity is in Section 2.7.

## Negotiating Tips: Licensor

- ***Scope.*** Are you willing to promise Licensee exclusivity? If Licensee is sharing revenues from Licensee's Site, Licensee may demand exclusivity. If you are willing to promise it, define what exclusivity means. For example, are you prohibited from providing links to named sites or any site owned by a competitor of Licensee? Are you required to take action if a third party who competes with Licensee links to your site without permission?

- ***Position of the Link.*** Section 2.1 requires you to place the Licensee's Image on your home page so that it is immediately visible by a user. You may not want to promise this placement: After all, there's a limit to how many "first view" links you can place on your home page. You may want to promise a link "deeper" in your site, or provide for rotating display of the Licensee's Image (see Form 7, the Advertising Contract for a discussion of display options).

- ***Appearance of Licensee's Image.*** Section 2.1 states how the Licensee's Image must appear to users of your Web site. If you are reluctant to undertake this level of commitment because of the limitations the commitment will impose on you, revise the provision.

- ***Control of Linked Site.*** If you are concerned about being linked to sites with inappropriate content (for example, pornographic sites, or sites furthering racist principles), you must decide how much control you wish to exercise over the Licensee's Site. Are you concerned only about content on Licensee's Site, or are you also concerned about the content on Web sites linked to Licensee's Site? In Section 3.4 (d), Licensee warrants that its site does not include inappropriate material. Section 3.3 gives you the right to terminate the agreement if Licensee materially alters the content or structure of Licensee's Site. You might also want the right to terminate the agreement if Licensee links to sites you deem inappropriate. According to Section 3.6 (b), Licensee must inform you of sites to which it is linked.

- ■ ***Compensation.*** In this agreement, your compensation for providing a link to Licensee's Site is a percentage of the advertising revenues from Licensee's Site (Section 1.8 and 4.1) based on the number of impressions by users coming to Licensee's site through the link. This form of compensation requires careful monitoring of Impressions by Licensee or a third party in order to ensure accurate records and payment. Section 3.5 states that records of Impressions must be maintained by a third party, but you may be willing to have Licensee perform the monitoring.

- ■ ***Availability of Licensed Site.*** If you are being paid a percentage of the advertising revenues generated by Licensee's Site, as this agreement provides, you will want the advertising revenues to be substantial. To maximize advertising revenues, Licensee's Site must be "up" (i.e. available) as long as possible and viewable by the greatest number of different types of browsers. Section 3.6 is a commitment by Licensee to use reasonable commercial efforts to keep its site "up" 24 hours a day, seven days a week.

- ■ ***Definition of Advertising Revenues.*** Advertising revenues is defined in Section 1.1 as gross revenue from advertising "invoiced" (not collected) by Licensee for advertising on Licensee's Site, less any commissions. Licensee's collection problems should not be your problem.

- ■ ***Liability for Licensee's Acts.*** It is unclear at this time what liability you might have for copyright infringement or other wrongs on Licensee's Site (such as the sale of defective products). Licensee's warranty and indemnity provisions, Sections 3.4 and 3.7, are designed to protect you from liability. However, the indemnity is worthless if Licensee does not have assets.

## Negotiating Tips: Licensee

- ■ ***Position of the Image.*** The placement of Licensee's Image on Licensor's Site is of critical importance to you: The more visible Licensee's Image is, the greater the likelihood that it will "drive" traffic to your site. Section 2.1 requires that the link be on the Licensor's home page and that it be immediately visible to users of the home page. Depending on the nature of your product or service, you might prefer to have the Licensor's Image on a different page on Licensor's Site—for example, one that gives information of particular interest to the type of consumer who would be interested in the products advertised on your site.

- ■ *Control of Site Content.* Web sites change, and you want to ensure that you can terminate this agreement if Licensor's Site changes so much that it no longer has the content or other features that made it attractive to you. Section 2.3 gives you this right. You also may want to have more control over the content on Licensor's Site, perhaps by obtaining from Licensor the same warranties you give in Section 3.4 (d), and over links to or from Licensor's Site.

## LINKING AGREEMENT

THIS AGREEMENT ("Agreement") is entered into by and between _____ (the "Licensor") and ___(the "Licensee") on the _____ (the "Effective Date").

RECITALS

WHEREAS, Licensor maintains a Web site relating to _____ at the following URL: http://_____;

WHEREAS, Licensee maintains a Web site at the following URL: http://_____;

WHEREAS, Licensee wishes to obtain a graphic link on Licensor's Web site which users of Licensor's Web site can click on to move to Licensee's Web site; and

WHEREAS, Licensor is willing to provide a graphic link on its Web site for Licensee, in consideration for receiving part of the advertising revenue generated by Licensee's Web site;

NOW, THEREFORE, in consideration of the promises and mutual covenants and agreements set forth herein, the parties agree as follows:

### Section 1
### Definitions

1.1 **Advertising Revenue** means the gross revenue from advertising invoiced by Licensee in a calendar quarter for advertising by third parties on the Licensee's Site, less any commissions.

1.2 **Impressions** means the loading of all or part of a Web page of the Licensee's Site into the browser of an User.

1.3 **Licensee's Home Page** means the home page of Licensee's Site located at URL: http://_____.

1.4 **Licensee's Image** means the graphic image listed on **Exhibit A**.

1.5 **Licensee's Site** means the Web site located at URL: http://_____.

1.6 **Licensor's Home Page** means the home page of Licensor's Site located at URL: http://_____.

1.7 **Licensor's Site** means the Web site located at URL: http://_____.

1.8 **Licensor's AR Share** means the number of Impressions on the Licensee's Site by Users arriving through the Link in a calendar quarter divided by the total number of Impressions on Licensee's Site by all Users in that calendar quarter.

1.9 **Link** means the hyperlink from Licensor's Site to Licensee's Site, as described in **Exhibit A**.

1.10 **User** means a person using a software browser to view the World Wide Web.

### Section 2
### Licensor's Obligations

2.1 **Placement of Link.** Licensor shall place the Licensee's Image on the upper right hand corner of the Licensor's Home Page so that the Licensee's Image is immediately visible by a User when loaded into the Netscape Navigator Version 2.0 and Microsoft's Internet Exchange Version 2.0 on a standard VGA monitor at 640 by 480 resolution when the browser is running in full screen configuration. In such configuration, the Licensee's Image shall not be less than __ pixels by __ pixels in size. The Licensee Image shall be visible by the User when the User first loads the Licensor's Home Page. The Licensee's Image when clicked by a User's mouse will move the User from Licensor's Site to Licensee's Site.

2.2 **User Information.** Licensor shall collect the following information on Users to Licensor's Site who use the Link: IP address and, if possible, name, address, salary, profession and other personal information ("Licensor User Information"). Licensor shall give notice to the Users that all Licensor User Information may be disclosed and used by other parties in the manner required by the most restrictive laws relating to the use of such personal information in the United States, the countries of the European Union, Japan, Canada, and Australia. Licensor shall provide a copy of the Licensor User Information collected during a calendar month to Licensee within thirty (30) days of the last day of the calendar month. Licensor shall use the Licensee User Information (defined in Section 3.2) solely for its internal business and marketing purposes.

2.3 **Licensor's Site Content.** Licensor acknowledges that the Link is based on the content of the Licensor's Site on the Effective Date. Licensee may terminate the Agreement if Licensor materially alters the content or structure of the Licensor's Site. Licensor shall give notice to Licensee of any material change in the content or structure of the Licensor's Site.

2.4 **Representations and Warranties.** Licensor represents and warrants that on the Effective Date and during the term of the Agreement:

(a) Licensor has the right to enter into this Agreement, and this Agreement does not conflict with any other agreement or obligation by which Licensor is bound.

(b) Licensor's Site does not violate the rights of any third parties in any jurisdiction, including without limitation, copyright, trademark, trade secret, privacy, publicity or other rights.

(c) Licensor's Site does not violate the laws, statutes, or regulations of any jurisdiction.

(d) Licensor disclaims all implied warranties, including without limitation, the warranties of merchantability, non-infringement of third party rights, and fitness for a particular purpose.

2.5 **Impressions.** Licensor and its employees shall not take actions which will artificially increase the number of Impressions on the Licensee's Site arriving through the Link. For example, Licensor's employees shall not repeatedly access the Licensee's Site through the Link.

2.6 **Retention of Rights.** Except as expressly licensed under this Agreement, Licensor retains all rights in Licensor's Site, its trademarks, copyrights, and intellectual property rights.

2.7 **Indemnification.** Licensor agrees to defend, indemnify, and hold harmless Licensee, its officers, directors, employees and agents, from and against any claims, actions, or demands, including without limitation reasonable legal and accounting fees, alleging or resulting from the breach of the warranties in Section 2.4. Licensee shall provide notice to Licensor promptly of any such claim, suit, or proceeding and shall assist Licensor, at Licensor's expense, in defending any such claim, suit, or proceeding.

## Section 3
## Licensee's Obligations

3.1 **Placement of Link.** Licensee shall place the Link from the Licensee's Image described in Section 2.1 on Licensee's Home Page. Licensee may not place the Link on a page that automatically reloads or goes to another page without further interaction from the User.

3.2 **User Information.** Licensee shall collect the following information on Users to Licensee's Site who arrive using the Link: IP address and, if possible, name, address, salary, profession and other personal information ("Licensee User Information"). Licensee shall give notice to the Users that all Licensee User Information may be disclosed and used by other parties in the manner required by the most restrictive laws relating to the use of such personal information in the United States, the countries of the European Union, Japan, Canada, and Australia. Licensee shall provide a copy of the Licensee User Information collected during a calendar month within thirty (30) days of the last day of the calendar month. Licensee shall use the Licensor User Information (defined in Section 2.2) solely for its internal business and marketing purposes.

3.3 **Licensee's Site Content.** Licensee acknowledges that this Agreement was made based on the content of the Licensee's Site on the Effective Date. Licensor may terminate the Agreement if Licensee materially alters the content or structure of the Licensee's Site. Licensee shall give notice to Licensor of any material change in the content or structure of the Licensee's Site.

3.4 **Representations and Warranties.** Licensee represents and warrants that on the Effective Date and during the term of the Agreement:

(a) Licensee has the right to enter into this Agreement, and this Agreement does not conflict with any other agreement or obligation by which Licensee is bound.

(b) Licensee's Site does not violate the rights of any third parties in any jurisdiction, including without limitation, copyright, trademark, trade secret, privacy, publicity, or other rights.

(c) Licensee's Site does not violate the laws, statutes or regulations of any jurisdiction.

(d) Licensee's Site does not include any material which is harmful, pornographic, abusive, hateful, obscene, threatening, or defamatory or which encourages illegal activities or racism or promotes software or services which deliver unsolicited email.

(e) Licensee's Site does not contain links to sites displaying the type of material defined in Section 3.4 (d) through a single connection.

(f) Licensee disclaims all implied warranties, including without limitation, the warranties of merchantability, non-infringement of third party rights, and fitness for a particular purpose.

## Section 6
## GOVERNING LAW AND DISPUTE RESOLUTION

6.1 **Arbitration.** The parties agree to submit any dispute arising out of or in connection with this Agreement to binding arbitration in _____ before the American Arbitration Association pursuant to the provisions of this Section 6.1, and, to the extent not inconsistent with this Section 6.1, the rules of the American Arbitration Association. The parties agree that such arbitration will be in lieu of either party's rights to assert any claim, demand or suit in any court action, (provided that either party may elect either binding arbitration or a court action with respect to obtain injunctive relief to terminate the violation by the other party of such party's proprietary rights, including without limitation any trade secrets, copyrights or trademarks). Any arbitration shall be final and binding and the arbitrator's order will be enforceable in any court of competent jurisdiction.

6.2 **Governing Law; Venue.** The validity, construction, and performance of this Agreement shall be governed by the laws of the state of _____, not including its conflicts of law principles, and all claims and/or lawsuits in connection with agreement must be brought in _____.

## Section 7
## MISCELLANEOUS PROVISIONS

7.1 **Notices.** For purposes of all notices and other communi cations required or permitted to be given hereunder, the addresses of the parties hereto shall be as indicated below. All notices shall be in writing and shall be deemed to have been duly given if sent by facsimile, the receipt of which is confirmed by return facsimile, or sent by first class registered or certified mail or equivalent, return receipt requested, addressed to the parties at their addresses set forth below:

If to Licensor:

_____

_____

_____

Attn: _____

If to Licensee:

_____

_____

_____

Attn: _____

7.2 **Entire Agreement.** This Agreement, including the attached Exhibits which are incorporated herein by reference as though fully set out, contains the entire understanding and agreement of the parties with respect to the subject matter contained herein, supersedes all prior oral or written understandings and agreements relating thereto except as expressly otherwise provided, and may not be altered, modified or waived in whole or in part, except in writing, signed by duly authorized representatives of the parties.

7.3 **Force Majeure.** Neither party shall be held responsible for damages caused by any delay or default due to any contingency beyond its control preventing or interfering with performance hereunder.

7.4 **Severability.** If any provision of this Agreement shall be held by a court of competent jurisdiction to be contrary to any law, the remaining provisions shall remain in full force and effect as if said provision never existed.

7.5 **Assignment.** Neither party may sell, assign, or transfer their rights or obligations under the Agreement without the written consent of the other party. This Agreement shall inure to the benefit of the permitted successors and assigns.

7.6 **Waiver and Amendments.** No waiver, amendment, or modification of any provision of this Agreement shall be effective unless consented to by both parties in writing. No failure or delay by either party in exercising any rights, power, or remedy under this Agreement shall operate as a waiver of any such right, power, or remedy.

7.7 **Agency.** The parties are separate and independent legal entities. Nothing contained in this Agreement shall be deemed to constitute either Licensor or Licensee an agent, representative, partner, joint venturer or employee of the other party for any purpose. Neither party has the authority to bind the other or to incur any liability on behalf of the other, nor to direct the employees of the other.

7.8 **Limitation on Liability; Remedies.** EXCEPT AS PROVIDED IN SECTIONS 2.7 AND 3.7 ABOVE, NEITHER PARTY SHALL BE LIABLE TO THE OTHER PARTY FOR ANY INCIDENTAL, CONSEQUENTIAL, SPECIAL, OR PUNITIVE DAMAGES OF ANY KIND OR NATURE, INCLUDING, WITHOUT LIMITATION, THE BREACH OF THIS AGREEMENT OR ANY TERMINATION OF THIS AGREEMENT, WHETHER SUCH LIABILITY IS ASSERTED ON THE BASIS OF CONTRACT, TORT (INCLUDING NEGLIGENCE OR STRICT LIABILITY), OR OTHERWISE, EVEN IF EITHER PARTY HAS WARNED OR BEEN WARNED OF THE POSSIBILITY OF ANY SUCH LOSS OR DAMAGE.

7.9 **Survival.** The obligations in Sections 2.4, 2.7, 3.4, 3.7, and 4.3 as well as the right to use certain personal information in Sections 2.2 and 3.2 shall survive termination of this Agreement.

IN WITNESS WHEREOF, this Agreement is executed as of the Effective Date set forth above.

[Licensor]                                          [Licensee]

By: _____     By: _____

       _____           _____
             Name                                                  Name

Its: _____     Its: _____
        Title                                                      Title

## EXHIBIT A
## LINK AND LICENSEE'S IMAGE

## EXHIBIT B
## LIST OF LINKS TO LICENSEE'S SITE

# FORM 12

# Domain Name Assignment Agreement

BY EARLY 1997, AN ESTIMATED 650,000 Internet Web sites were pumping content out into cyberspace. This is a dramatic increase since 1996 when approximately 100,000 Web sites were operating. At least 49 million users (40 million of those in the United States) on 240,000 interconnected computer networks now use the Internet. The number of Internet users grows at more than 150 percent per year, and 60 percent of the new users are commercial users. Clearly, the Internet is much, much more than the CB radio of the nineties.

To have a presence in the Internet community, you must select and register a unique domain name. A domain name is your metaphorical street address on the Internet and is necessitated by the architecture of the Internet. This architecture is premised upon each machine connected to the Internet being uniquely identifiable. A unique "Internet Protocol" address is assigned to each Internet machine. This IP Address is a cross between a postal address and a telephone number comprising four

---

This chapter, written by Jason D. Firth and Katherine C. Spelman, does not reflect the opinions of Mark Radcliffe or of Gray, Cary, Ware & Freidenrich or its clients.

Jason D. Firth
Katherine C. Spelman
Steinhart & Falconer
333 Market Street,
32nd Floor
San Francisco, CA
94105-2150
Telephone:
  (415) 777-3999
Facsimile:
  (415) 442-0856 or
  (415) 442-0839
E-Mail:
  JDF@Steinhart.com
  KCS@Steinhart.com

groups of up to three digit numbers. A typical IP Address is 768.403.2.189. You can be connected to the Internet using only an IP Address. IP Addresses can be obtained easily at no charge. However, IP Addresses are difficult to remember and a custom has developed of using domain names, which are words and abbreviations that are easier to remember than a string of numbers. These domain names, in turn, represent an IP Address which can change over time. Another advantage of domain names is that they remain the same even if you change your IP Address (for example, by changing your Internet Service Provider).

A domain name address generally has two parts: a top level domain name and a second level domain name (you also can include a "third" and "fourth" level domain name). In an Internet address (technically known as a "uniform resource locator" or URL), the top level domain name is found farthest to the right after the "dot." For example, in "adobe.com", the "adobe" is a second level domain and ".com" is the top level domain. The top level domain is a suffix and is managed by one of the more than 100 domain name registries. Current top level domain names include two main types: "global" top level domains such as .com, .edu, .org, and .net; and "geographic" top level domains such as .us (United States), .uk (United Kingdom), .fr (France), and .de (Germany).

The second level domain name is a name chosen by the registrant who can pick any combination of 22 characters or less that are not already registered. Many companies use their most famous trademark as a second level domain name.

The combination of the top level and the second level domain address results in domain names such as these:

| Domain Name | Domain Name Registrant |
|---|---|
| Disney.com | The Walt Disney Company |
| UNICEF.org | United Nations Children's Fund |
| BBC.co.uk | British Broadcasting Corporation |
| WhiteHouse.gov | Executive Office of the President of the USA |

These domain names then are incorporated into URLs and email addresses such as these:

| Internet Address | Internet Resource |
|---|---|
| http://www.disney.com/Disneyland/index.html | The Disneyland Web site |
| president@whitehouse.gov | Bill Clinton's email address |

## Geographic Domain Names

Each country connected to the Internet has its own top level domain names. These top level domains correspond to the internationally recognized country abbreviations such as .uk, .us, .ja, and .fr. Geographic top level domain names are registered by an organization in each country that has been delegated this responsibility. In some countries, the registry will be operated by a university; in some, a government agency; and in some, a private company. The .us registry is administered by the University of Southern California. Most countries have sub-registries broken down by the type of entity or location. For example, commercial entities in the United Kingdom can use the top level domain name .co.uk. Often these domain names can end up being long and cumbersome such as alpine.k12.ut.us, the top level domain name for primary schools in the Alpine school district of Utah.

For more information about the .us domain name registry, contact the Web site at http://www.isi.edu:80/in-notes/usdnr/

The following Web sites contain links to the other geographic domain name registries around the world:

http://rs.internic.net/help/other-reg.html
http://www.uninett.no/navn/domreg.html

## Global Domain Names

There are four global top level domain names for use by entities regardless of their location. These domain names and their intended holders are:

.com    commercial entities
.net    computer network providers
.int    organizations established by international treaties and international databases
.org    miscellaneous organizations such as nonprofits

Except for .int, these global domain names are administered by another company, Network Solutions Inc., operating as a joint venture under the name InterNIC and under a contract from the National Science Foundation. Three other global top level domains, .edu, .gov and .mil, are limited to use in the United States. These global domain names are by far the most popular domain names, especially in the United States. Among them, .com is the most sought after. As of February 1997, there were 954,139 registrations for .com as compared to 63,807 for .org and 58,099 for .net. Because of the importance of the global domain names administered by InterNIC, most of the remainder of this chapter will deal specifically with InterNIC registrations.

## Possible Changes

Many ideas have been raised to resolve the competition for the most desirable global domain names and to reduce the control U.S. entities have over such domain names. The most influential proposal to date was authored by the International Ad Hoc Committee (IAHC). IAHC's "Memorandum of Understanding" proposes establishing seven new top level domain names (.firm, .store, .web, .arts, .rec, .info, .nom) with new registries throughout the world. It also proposes an international dispute resolution process. It is not clear yet whether the IAHC proposal will be implemented. More information regarding the IAHC and its proposal can be found at http://www.gtld-mou.org

## Domain Name Disputes

As mentioned, the global domain names administered by InterNIC are by far the most popular. As a result, disputes involving competing claims to domain names are increasingly common. Indeed, since 1994 there have been more than 40 such disputes reported in the media.

Most of these disputes have involved the dispute resolution policy established by InterNIC. By understanding the basics of InterNIC's policy, you can better understand how to select and protect domain names and why domain name transfers are often important.

## Network Solutions Dispute Resolution Policy

Initially, InterNIC registered domain names purely on a first-come-first-served basis. Under that policy, a reporter unaffiliated with McDonalds Corporation was able to register "mcdonalds.com" and an MTV television personality registered "mtv.com" in their own names. Of course, the McDonalds Corporation and MTV Networks objected. In light of these and other well-publicized cases, InterNIC modified its policy in hopes of avoiding additional disputes.

Under the current InterNIC policy, while you may still register with InterNIC a domain name that has not been previously registered, your name can later be challenged. To challenge a domain name, the "challenger" presents InterNIC with a certified copy of a United States or foreign trademark registration certificate for a name which is "identical" to the second level domain name. InterNIC then looks to the respective date the domain name was acquired and the dates reflected in the challenger's trademark registration certificate. If the domain name was secured before the "effective" date of the registration (either the date of registration or the date of first use of the challenger's trademark as reflected in the registration certificate depending on the country), the domain name holder is free to continue using the domain name and InterNIC will take no action.

On the other hand, if the challenger's trademark registration or first use predates the domain name application, then the domain name holder must produce its own U.S. or foreign trademark registration, establishing that it owns a trademark registration "identical" to its second level domain name. If so, the domain name holder is free to continue using the domain name and InterNIC will take no action. When the domain name holder cannot do so, InterNIC will ask the holder to relinquish the domain name to the challenger. A domain name holder can select a new domain name and use both domain names for up to 90 days. If a holder refuses to relinquish its domain name, InterNIC will bar both the holder and the challenger from using the name until the dispute is resolved in court, arbitration, or settlement.

Despite InterNIC's efforts to draft a comprehensive policy, many questions remain with respect to domain name registration and protection, such as what constitutes "identical" trademark registration. More broadly, questions remain about the fairness of the policy. For example, under U.S. trademark law a company can acquire rights in a trademark merely by using the mark to promote its goods or services. Yet InterNIC's policy appears to provide a remedy only for federally registered trademarks.

Similarly, the law remains unsettled as to what standards should apply in finding a conflict between a trademark and a domain name. Trademark law rests on the concept of confusion; that is, trademark infringement occurs only when two companies use the same or similar marks on the same or similar goods so that a consumer may be confused as to the source of the goods. InterNIC's policy, however, is not concerned with the goods or services offered under the name at issue. In one recent case, Warner Bros. attempted to use its trademark registration for "Road Runner" to suspend use of the domain name "roadrunner.com" by a New Mexico Internet Service Provider, even though the ISP had been using "Roadrunner Software" as its company name for many years and even though the domain name was not used in connection with entertainment services.

## Establishing Strong Domain Name Rights

Despite the uncertainty, one thing remains clear—domain name disputes are costly and disruptive. Since the law is still developing, litigation in this area is expensive. Names have been purchased as a means of settlement, but the cost may run to hundreds of thousands of dollars. Having to change an established domain name could result in a variety of harms, from lost sales and customer confusion to printing costs for changing business cards and advertising.

Under current law, you can minimize the likelihood of a domain name dispute by taking these steps:

### 1. Conduct Trademark Searches

After you select a potential domain name, you should have a full trademark search conducted to determine whether the domain name could violate another's rights. Even if you have already adopted a domain name, you should consider a trademark search regarding the name to assess the risk of a dispute. Keep in mind that the traditional trademark standard—likelihood of confusion—may not govern in domain name disputes. Even if another company has a trademark registered for goods or services entirely different from those you provide, that company could possibly object to your use of a domain name identical to its trademark.

### 2. Register Trademarks Corresponding to Domain Names

Aside from the other benefits of trademark registration, InterNIC grants domain name holders owning trademark registrations identical to their domain names the presumptive right to use the names. Accordingly, any name you are using or intend to use as a domain name that is capable of being registered as a trademark should be registered. Names are capable of trademark registration if they are not generic terms for the goods or services involved (e.g., BIKE is generic for bicycles but not for gym clothes) and if they are used to promote the goods or services involved.

### 3. Register Domain Names Early

Domain names are still obtained in the first instance on a first-come-first-served basis. The first to register a name has the right to use it unless another can prove superior rights. Thus, you should select and register domain names as soon as possible. If you wait too long, you may find a competitor has hamstrung you by registering domain names corresponding to your company or product names, or you may have to purchase a domain name from a "pirate" such as the company that recently announced it would sell domain names including "wallstreet.org", "gratefuldead.org", or "videodating.com" for up to $375,000.

You should consider registering domain names that correspond to your company name, the trademarks used with your company's goods or services, and the generic names for your company's goods or services. You also should consider registering more than one domain name. If a dispute arises with one name, you will have a backup name ready to use. To find out if a particular domain name is available, access InterNIC's "Whois" service at http://rs.internic.net/cgi-bin/whois.

The process for registering a domain name is simple. First you must be connected to the Internet. For most businesses, it means contracting with an Internet service provider (ISP), since InterNIC will not register a domain name until you have the infrastructure in place to use it. A list of ISPs, searchable by name and location, is available at http://thelist.iworld.com. The list provides information about each ISP's services and price structure as well as contact information. Most ISPs will register a domain name for you or you can do it yourself by submitting a form (available at http://rs.internic.net/help/templates.html) and paying a $100 fee for a two-year registration. Remember that these rules are for the InterNIC registry and different rules apply to the national registries.

When registering a domain name, be careful about what or who listed as the owner. It should be whatever entity owns your organization's other assets (e.g., the parent corporation), not the ISP or an individual or a company division. Also make sure that the administrative contact on the registration is someone trustworthy because he or she will have great power over your registration. Listing two administrative contacts is advisable in case one should become unavailable.

## Domain Name Transfers

Often it is necessary to transfer a domain name from one entity to another. For example, to complete a corporate acquisition or merger, to resolve a domain name dispute, or to correct a situation where a domain name is registered in the name of an ISP rather than the actual user of the name. Transferring a domain name registered with InterNIC, requires the following steps:

1. Do a "whois" search to determine the registration status of the domain name. The registration should be current with all fees paid before attempting a transfer.

2. The Administrative Contact listed in the registration of the Transferor should complete a registration template (available at http://rs.internic.net/help/templates.html) requesting deletion of the domain name. The Administrative Contact should then email the completed template to the Transferee with a subject line reading "Transfer Domain Name _____" (specifying the domain name).

    2a. If the Administrative Contact listed in the registration of the Transferor is unavailable or no longer has access to the Internet from the email address listed in the registration, the Transferor should send a letter to InterNIC via facsimile at 703-742-9552. The letter should be on the Transferor's official letterhead and should be signed by the Transferor (if an individual) or an officer of the Transferor (if a corporation). The letter's signer should state his or her title and authority to legally bind the Transferor, enclose a photocopy of his or her driver's license, include the signer's daytime phone number, and authorize transfer of the domain name to the Transferee.

3. The Transferee should then complete a registration template requesting a new registration. The Transferee should email the new registration template to InterNIC at HOSTMASTER@INTERNIC.NET. If the Transferor prepared a deletion template, it should be appended to the new registration template. The email header from both parties should be intact to provide evidence of appropriate authorization.

Detailed instructions on transferring domain names registered with InterNIC are available at http://rs.internic.net/help/xferreg.html.

The form below may be used to memorialize an agreement to transfer a domain name. The provisions numbered 1 and 3 are optional.

# DOMAIN NAME ASSIGNMENT AGREEMENT

**WHEREAS** [transferring party], [a _____ corporation having a principal place of business at _____][an individual residing at _____] ("Transferor"), has adopted, used and registered with InterNIC [or other domain name registry] the domain name _____ (the "Domain Name");
and

**WHEREAS** [receiving party], [a _____ corporation having a principal place of business at _____][an individual residing at _____] ("Transferee"), is desirous of acquiring the Domain Name and the registration therefor;

**NOW THEREFORE**, for good and valuable consideration, receipt of which is hereby acknowledged, Transferor hereby transfers and assigns to Transferee all of Transferor's right, title and interest in and to the Domain Name and the registration therefor.

**FURTHERMORE,** the Parties agree as follows:

1. Transferee agrees to pay Transferor _____ dollars, payable [upon execution of this agreement] [upon completion of the transfer of the Domain Name].

2. Transferor agrees to cooperate with Transferee and to follow Transferee's instructions in order to effectuate the transfer of the Domain Name registration in a timely manner. Specifically, Transferor agrees to prepare and transmit the necessary InterNIC registration deletion template and/or to correspond with InterNIC to authorize transfer of the Domain Name.

3. Transferor warrants and represents that:

    (a) Transferor has unencumbered rights in the Domain Name;

    (b) Transferor properly registered the Domain Name with InterNIC without committing fraud or misrepresentation;

    (c) Transferor has the authority to transfer the Domain Name;

    (d) Transferor has not received any claim from a third party that the use of Domain Name violates the rights of such third party;

    (e) Transferor has not used the Domain Name for any illegal purpose; and

    (f) to the best of Transferor's knowledge, the use of the Domain Name does not infringe the rights of any third party in any jurisdiction.

4. This agreement is governed by the internal substantive laws of the State of _____. If any provision of this agreement is found to be invalid by any court having competent jurisdiction, the invalidity of such provision shall not affect the validity of the remaining provisions of this agreement, which shall remain in full force and effect. No waiver of any term of this agreement shall be deemed a further or continuing waiver of such term or any other term. This agreement constitutes the entire agreement between the Transferor and Transferee with respect to this transaction. Any changes to this agreement must be made in writing, signed by an authorized representative of both parties.

**IN WITNESS WHEREOF,** the Parties have caused this document to be executed by their authorized officers on the date(s) indicated below.

**Form 12**

Transferor

By _____

Name _____

Title _____

Date _____

Transferee

By _____

Name _____

Title _____

Date _____

## Additional Sample Contracts!
# MULTIMEDIA CONTRACTS

**Actual Contracts from the Multimedia Industry**

**Over 600 pages—56 full agreements (also available on disk)**

Ladera Press also publishes *Multimedia Contracts*, a 600-page book with 56 contracts that actually have been used in the multimedia industry. The first book of its kind, it includes all types of multimedia contracts from personal releases to development agreements to publishing agreements. These contracts are not available elsewhere. The contracts in *Multimedia Contracts* have been submitted by well-known lawyers and companies in the multimedia industry. The book includes agreements submitted by Jeremy Salesin, General Counsel of Sanctuary Woods, and by Ian Rose, General Counsel of Mindscape, Inc. The book has been endorsed by the Interactive Multimedia Association, the largest and oldest multimedia trade association.

## What you'll find in Multimedia Contracts:

- Releases for individuals and locations
- Music licenses such as a recording artist license and the Warner/Chappell Synch license, content and software licenses
- Production agreements including an actor's agreement, director's agreement, and writer's agreement
- Eleven publishing agreements, including two used by Philips Interactive Media
- Eight development contracts
- On-line services agreement from a major on-line information service
- Eight software escrow agreements
- Interactive agreements from SAG, AFTRA, and Writers Guild
- Copyright assignments, including some specifically designed for screenplays
- Work for hire and independent contractor agreements

The price of the *Multimedia Contracts* book is $89.95 plus $7 shipping
(plus 8.25% sales tax for California residents).

The actual contracts also are available on diskette (IBM or MAC) for $99.95
(U.S. shipping included).

Shipping to Canada or Mexico is $9. Shipping to other foreign countries is $25.

To order by phone, have your Mastercard or Visa handy and call (800) 523-3721.
Or order by mail or fax using the order form at the end of this book.

*The Essential Guide To Internet
And Multimedia Legal Issues*

# Multimedia Law and Business Handbook

Need more information on the legal issues covered in this book's Overview of Internet legal issues?

*Multimedia Law and Business Handbook* is the answer. This 468-page book includes chapters on copyright law, copyright ownership, other intellectual property laws, licensing, entertainment industry unions, educational issues, and special Internet legal issues.

Like the Overview, it includes numerous examples to show how the law is applied in particular situations as well as checklists and sample agreements.

The price of the book is $44.95 plus $7 shipping (plus 8.25% sales tax for California residents). Shipping to Canada or Mexico is $9 per book. Shipping to other foreign countries is $25 per book (U.S. Mail, Air Mail Book rate).

- **To order by phone,** have your Mastercard or Visa handy and call (800) 523-3721.

- **To order by mail or fax,** use the order form at the end of this book.

- **UPS 2nd Day Air delivery is available**: For delivery in the continental United States, add $10 to the regular shipping fee. For delivery to Alaska or Hawaii, add $15 to the regular shipping fee.

## Need Additional Copies?

Additional copies of *Internet Legal Forms for Business* are available for $24.95 plus $5 shipping (California residents, add 8.25% sales tax).

Shipping to Canada and Mexico is $6. Shipping to other foreign countries is $15.

## Need a diskette?

The forms in this book are available on diskette (PC only) for $12 (California residents add 8.25%).

Specify the *Internet Legal Forms for Business Diskette* when ordering. U.S. shipping is included in the price. For shipping to Canada or Mexico, add $2. For shipping to other foreign countries, add $10.

- **Orders**: To order by phone, have your credit card handy and call (800) 523-3721. Or order by mail or fax using the order form at the end of this book.

- For delivery by UPS 2nd Day Air: For delivery in the continental United States, add $10 to the regular shipping fee. For delivery to Alaska or Hawaii, add $15 to the regular shipping fee.

- **Comments?** We are interested in your comments and suggestions on how to improve this book. Please send them to us by mail, email, or fax at the following addresses:

Ladera Press
3130 Alpine Road
Suite 200-9002
Menlo Park, Ca. 94205

email: Laderapres@aol.com

fax: (650) 854-0642

**Coming In Summer, 1998**

# Internet Law And Business Handbook

*Internet Law and Business Handbook*, due out in the summer of 1998, will be a comprehensive, practical guide to the legal and business issues that arise in various aspects of using the Internet.

Designed for the nonlawyer, this book will contain clear explanations of the applicable laws and numerous examples to help you understand how these laws apply to real-world situations.

Appropriate for both experienced and novice Internet users, the book will include an introduction to the Internet and "building block" chapters on copyright law, patent law, trademark law, trade secret law, and contracts law. It will include also chapters on the following topics:

- *Posting material on the Internet*
  Using Pre-existing Content ● Clearing Rights and Obtaining Licenses
  Using Music Online ● Publicity, Privacy, and Defamation Online
- *Creating Material for the Internet*
  Web Development Agreements ● Employees, Contractors and Consultants
- *Taking Material from the Internet*
- *Internet Commerce*
  Internet Business Strategies ● Choosing Domain Names and Products
  Payment Systems, Export Control Laws, Sales Law

The price of the book is $34.95 plus $7 shipping (plus 8.25% sales tax for California residents). Shipping to Canada or Mexico is $9 per book. Shipping to other foreign countries is $9 per book.

- **To order by phone**, have your Mastercard or Visa handy and call (800) 523-3721.
- **To order by mail or fax,** use the order form at the end of this book.
- **UPS 2nd Day Air delivery is available**: For delivery in the continental United States, add $10 to the regular shipping fee. For delivery to Alaska or Hawaii, add $15 to the regular shipping fee.

# Ladera Press Order form

Use this form to order additional Ladera Press products described on the immediately preceding pages.

TO ORDER BY MAIL: Complete the form and mail to:
Ladera Press
c/o Port City Fulfillment
250 Huron Ave.
Port Huron, MI 48060
TO ORDER BY FAX: Complete the form and fax to (810) 987-3562.
TO ORDER BY PHONE: Have your credit card handy and call (800) 523-3721.

Name _____

Title _____ Email address: _____

Company _____

Address _____

City _____ State _____ Zip _____

Telephone _____ Fax _____

Method of payment:   ❏ Check enclosed     ❏ Visa        ❏ Mastercard

Type of diskette needed:   ❏ PC      ❏ Macintosh

   Credit Card Account Number: _____

            Expiration Date: _____

               Signature _____

| Quantity | Item | Price | Total |
|---|---|---|---|
|  |  |  |  |
|  |  |  |  |
|  |  |  |  |
|  |  |  |  |
|  |  |  |  |
|  | Subtotal |  |  |
|  | 8.25% Sales Tax (CA Residents) |  |  |
|  | Shipping (see preceding pages) |  |  |
|  | UPS 2nd Day $10/$15 |  |  |
|  | TOTAL |  |  |

Please allow 2–3 weeks for delivery.